The Story of the Holy Prophet

(Peace Be Upon Them)

Ibn Kathir

Copyright ©
King Fahd Complex for the Printing
Editor: Al-Imam Ahmad

Prophet Adam
The Father of Mankind

After God created the sun, the moon, the planets, and all the stars—billions of them! God told the angels that He was going to create a man. The Angeles asked, "Will You make someone who will cause mischief and kill?" God said to the Angels, "I know what you do not know."

God then created the first man, Adam, from dust (wet clay). God taught Adam the names of everything in His creation, including the sun, the moon, the stars, the plants, and the animals. Then God showed the same things to the Angels and God said, "Tell Me the names of these things if you are truthful!" The angels said, "glory to You, the Most High, we have no knowledge except what you have taught us. You are the All-Knowing, the All-Wise."

God then said, "O Adam, tell them the name of all things." After Adam told them the names, God told the Angels to bow down to Adam. They all bowed down, but amongst the angels was Satan, the Devil. Satan was a jinn, a being made of smokeless fire. Satan did not bow down with the angels to Adam and said, "I am better than this man. You made me from fire. But him you made from clay." Satan showed his envy and arrogance.

Adam was surprised by this creature, Satan who abhorred him without even knowing him and who imagined himself better than him without having proved that he was worthier.

God gives His commissioned creatures' absolute freedom even to the extent that they can refuse His commands. God grants them the freedom of denial, disobedience, and even disagreement with Him. His kingdom will not diminish if the disbelievers do not believe in Him nor will it be extended if many people believe in Him.

God ordered Satan to leave paradise, but Satan asked God to give him some time away from the punishment until the Day of Judgment. God granted Satan that time. Satan said that he would use his time to persuade all humans to sin, so they burn with him. Satan said that he would whisper temptations and evil ideas into their ears. He swore that only few humans would prove themselves grateful to God. Only God's most faithful servants would remember God.

God told Adam and his wife, Eve, to live in Paradise and to eat freely of the things there. However, there was only one tree that God warned them not to come near. But Satan was jealous, and he whispered over and over again to Adam and Eve. He persuaded them both to forget that they should be obedient to God. He tempted them to eat from the forbidden tree. Adam and Eve understood that they were forbidden to eat the fruit of that tree. Adam was, however, a human being, and man tends to forget. So Adam and Eve took the apple. Suddenly, after eating the fruit, they both felt ashamed. They gathered the leaves and branches from the Garden of Paradise and they tried to cover themselves. But God sees all things and they could not hide themselves or their sin from Him.

Adam and Eve felt very bad and sorry for what they had done. They asked God for His forgiveness and mercy. They remembered that they could not even live without His mercy. God forgave them and made Adam the first prophet on earth. God told Adam and Eve that whoever follows His guidance then should never be afraid, and after they die, they will return to paradise forever.

Human beings cannot see Satan. This is one key reason to pray so to remember God, and to ask God for wisdom and guidance.

Prophet Enoch (Idris)

A High Ranking Prophet

Prophet Adam and his wife Eve had many children. God made many of their children prophets. God's Book mentions Prophet Enoch (Idris) (peace be upon him). He was the great grandson of Adam's son, Seth. He was a man of truth, sincerity, and honesty, so God raised him to a high rank.

Prophet Encoh repeatedly called his people to worship God alone. But very few of his people listened to his call. Most of his people laughed and turned away.

Prophet Enoch taught the people to be honest and just. He taught them to pray and also to fast. He taught them to give a portion of their wealth to the poor.

Prophet Enoch taught his people many more important things. And he warned his people not to envy each other. He taught them that the best way to show gratitude for God's favors is to share them with others. He warned his people not to be excessive or extravagant because they would not benefit from it in the end. He told them that the real joy of life is to have wisdom and to do great deeds.

It was reported that Prophet David was a maker of shields. Prophet Adam was a farmer. Prophet Jesus and Noah were carpenters. Prophet Mohammad and Moses were shepherds. And Prophet Idris (Enoch) was a tailor. So Prophet Enoch is considered as the originator of his craft.

Prophet Noah (Nuh) and the Ark
A Faithful Servant

Noah was born 126 years after the death of Adam. There were some good men among Noah's people. However, after their deaths, statues of these men were built to keep their memories alive. However, after sometime, Noah's people began to worship these statues. Later generations did not even know why they had been built; they only knew their parents had prayed to them. That is how idol worshipping developed. Since they had no understanding of Allah the Almighty Who would punish them for their evil deeds, they became cruel and immoral.

Noah's people worshiped statues and they called gods. They believed that these gods would bring them good, protect them from evil and provide all their needs. They gave their idols names. These idols represented, respectively, manly power, mutability, beauty, brute strength, swiftness, sharp sight, insight, according to the power they thought these gods possessed.

So Satan had caused them to forget God. So prophets were sent when people went astray.

For many years and generations Noah's people had been worshipping statues that they called gods. They believed that these gods would bring them good, protect them from evil, and provide all their needs. These idols to them represented, manly power, beauty, brute strength, swiftness, sharp sight, and insight.

For example, Waddan was a righteous man who was loved by his people. When he died, they withdrew to his grave and were overwhelmed by sadness. When Satan saw their sorrow caused by his death, he disguised himself in the form of a man saying: 'I have seen your sorrow because of this man's death; can I make a statue like him which could be put in your meeting place to make you remember him?' They said: 'yes.' So Satan made the statue like him. They put it in their meeting place in order to be reminded of him.

When Satan saw their interest in remembering him, he said: 'Can I build a statue of him in the home of each one of you so that he would be in everyone's house and you could remember him?'

They agreed. Their children learned about and saw what they were doing. They also learned about their remembrance of him instead of God. So the first to be worshipped instead of Allah was Waddan, the idol which they named thus.

By worshipping anything other than Allah, man becomes enslaved to Satan. So Allah sent Noah with His message to his people. Noah was the only intelligent man that was not caught in worshiping idols. Noah was an excellent speaker and a very patient man.

He pointed out to his people the mysteries of life and the wonders of the universe. He pointed out how the night is regularly followed by the day and that the balance between these opposites were designed by God the Almighty for our good.

The night gives coolness and rest while the day gives warmth and awakens activity.

The sun encourages growth, keeping all plants and animals alive, while the moon and stars assist in the reckoning of time, direction and seasons. He pointed out that the ownership of the heavens and the earth belongs only to the Divine Creator.

Noah explained to this people, there cannot have been more than one deity (god). He explained to them how the devil had deceived them for so long and that the time had come for this deceit to stop. Noah told them that idol worshipping was wrong. He warned them not to worship anyone but God. Noah told them about the terrible punishment God would bring if they continued in their evil ways.

The people listened to him in silence. Noah's words touched the hearts of the weak, the poor, and the miserable and soothed their wounds with its mercy.

As for the rich, the strong, the mighty and the rulers they looked upon the warning with cold distrust. They believed they would be better off if things stayed the same. Therefore they started their war of words against Noah. First they accused Noah of being only human like themselves. The chiefs of the disbelievers among his people said: "We see you but a man like ourselves."' Noah, however, had never said anything other than that.

The contest between the polytheists and Noah continued. The rulers had thought at first that Noah's call would soon fade on its own. When they found that his call attracted the poor, the helpless and common laborers, they started to verbally attack and taunt him: 'You are only followed by the poor, the meek and the worthless.'

Thus the conflict between Noah and the heads of his people intensified. The disbelievers tried to bargain: "Listen Noah, if you want us to believe in you, then dismiss your believers. They are meek and poor, while are elite and rich; no faith can include us both."

Noah listened to the heathens of his community and realized they were being obstinate. However, he was gentle in his response. He explained to his people that he could not dismiss the believers as they were not his guests but Allah's guests.

Noah appealed to them: "O my people! I ask of you no wealth for it, my reward is from none but Allah. O my people! I do not say to you that with me are the Treasures of Allah nor that I know the unseen, nor do I say I am an angel. The rulers were tired of Noah's arguments. And they said: "O Noah! Bring upon us what you threaten us with, if you are of the truthful." He said: "Only Allah will bring the punishment on you."

Noah continued appealing to his people to believe in Allah hour after hour, day after day year after year. But whenever he called them to Allah, they ran away from him. Whenever he urged them to ask Allah to forgive them, they put their fingers in their ears and became too proud to listen to the truth.

Noah saw that the number of believers was not increasing, while that of the disbelievers was. He was sad for his people, but he never reached the point of despair. But there came a day when Allah revealed to Noah that no others would believe. Allah inspired him not to grieve for them at which point Noah prayed that the disbelievers be destroyed. Allah accepted Noah's prayer. The case was closed, and He passed His judgment on the disbelievers in the form of a flood.

Allah ordered Noah to build an ark with His knowledge and instructions and with the help of angels. Noah chose a place outside the city, far from the sea. He collected wood and tools and began to day and night to build the ark. The people's mockery continued: "Why are you building an ark so far from the sea? Are you going to drag it to the water or is the wind going to carry it for you?"

The ship was built, and Noah sat waiting for Allah's command. Allah revealed to him that when water miraculously gushed forth from the oven at Noah's house that would be the sign of the start of the flood, and the sign for Noah to act. The terrible day arrived when the oven at Noah's house overflowed. Noah hurried to open the ark and summon the believers. He also took with him a pair, male and female, of every type of animal, bird and insect. Seeing him taking these creatures to the ark, the people laughed loudly: "Noah must have gone out of his head! What is he going to do with the animals?"

Noah's wife was not a believer with him so she did not join him; neither did one of Noah's sons, who was secretly a disbeliever but had pretended faith in front of Noah.

The scholars hold different opinions on the number of those who were with Noah on the ship. Some said there were 80 believers, and others claimed that there were only 10 with Noah.

Water rose from the cracks in the earth; there was not a crack from which water did not rise. Rain poured from the sky in quantities never seen before on earth.

Water continued pouring from the sky rising from the cracks; hour after hour the level rose. The seas and waves invaded the land. The interior of the earth moved in a strange way, and the ocean floors lifted suddenly, flooding the dry land. The earth, for the first time was submerged. Then with the issue of the divine command, calm returned to earth, the water retreated, and the dry land shone once again in the rays of the sun. The flood had cleansed the earth of the disbelievers and polytheists. Noah released the birds and the animals.

After that the believers disembarked. Noah put his forehead to the ground in prayer. The survivors kindled a fire and sat around it. Lighting a fire had been prohibited on board so as not to ignite the ship's wood and burn it up. None of them had eaten hot food during the entire period of the floor. Following the disembarkation there was a day of fasting in thanks to Allah.

Allah's Book draws the curtain on Noah's story. We do not know what happened next. All we know is that on his deathbed Noah requested his son to worship Allah alone, Noah then passed away.

Prophet Hud and the Storm
A Trusting Servant

The people of Ad lived many years in the windswept hills of an area between Yemen and Oman. They were physically well built and renowned for their craftsmanship especially in the construction of tall buildings with lofty towers. They were outstanding among all the nations in power and wealth, which, unfortunately, made them arrogant and boastful. Their political power was held in the hand of unjust rulers, against whom no one dared to raise a voice.

They were not ignorant of the existence of God, nor did they refuse to worship Him. What they did refuse was to worship Allah (God) alone. They worshipped other gods, also, including idols. This is one sin God does not forgive.

God wanted to guide and discipline these people so He sent a prophet from among them. This prophet was Hud (peace be upon him), a noble man who handled this task with great resoluteness and tolerance.

Prophet Hud condemned idol worship and admonished his people. "MY people, what is the benefit of these stones that you carve with your own hands and worship? In reality it is an insult to the intellect. There is only One Deity worthy of worship and that is Allah. Worship Allah alone.

Allah created you, He provides for you and He is the One Who will cause you to die. He gave you wonderful physiques and blessed you in many ways. So believe in Him and do not be blind to His favors, or the same fate that destroyed Noah's people will overtake you."

With such reasoning Hud hoped to instill faith in them, but they refused to accept his message. His people asked him: "Do you desire to be our master with your call? What payment do you want?"

Hud tried to make them understand that he would receive his payment (reward) from Allah; he did not demand anything from them except that they let the light of truth touch their minds and hearts.

They said: "O Hud! No evidence have you brought us and we shall not leave our gods!"

Hud tried to speak to them and to explain about Allah's blessings: how Allah the Almighty had made them Noah's successors, how He had given them strength and power, and how He sent them rain to revive the soil.

Hud's people looked about them and found they were the strongest on earth, so they become prouder and more obstinate. Thus they argued a lot with Hud. They asked "O Hud! Do you say that later we die and turn into dust, we will be resurrected?" He replied, "Yes, you will come back on the Day of Judgment and each of you will be asked about what you did."

A peal of laughter was heard after the last statement. "How strange Hud's claims are!" They believed that when man dies his body decays and turns into dust, which is swept away by the wind. How could that return back to life? All their questions were patiently received by Prophet Hud. He then addressed his people concerning the Day of Judgment. He explained that belief in the Day of Judgment is essential to Allah's justice, teaching them the same thing that every prophet taught about it.

Hud explained that justice demands that there be a Day of Judgment because good is not always victorious in life. Sometimes evil overpowers good. Will such crimes go unpunished? If we suppose there is no Day of Judgment, then a great injustice will have prevailed, but Allah has forbidden injustice. Therefore, the existence of the Day of Judgment, a day of accounting for our deeds and being rewarded or punished for them, reveals the extend of Allah's justice. Hud spoke to them about all of these things. They listened but disbelieved him.

The chiefs of Hud's people asked: "Is it not strange that Allah's chooses one of us to reveal His message to?"

Hud replied: "What is strange in that? Allah wants to guide you to the right way of life, so He sent me to warn you.

Noah's flood and his story are not far away from you, so do not forget what happened. All the disbelievers were destroyed, no matter how strong they were."

"Who is going to destroy us Hud?" the chiefs asked. "Allah." replied Hud.

The disbelievers among his people answered: "We will be saved by our gods."

Prophet Hud clarified to them that the gods they worshipped would be the reason for their destruction, that it is Allah alone Who saves people, and that no other power on earth can benefit or harm anyone.

The conflict between Hud and his people continued. The years passed, and they became prouder and more obstinate, and more tyrannical and more defiant of their prophet's message.

Furthermore, they started to accuse Hud of being a crazy. One day they told him: "We now understand the secret of your madness you insulted our gods and they harmed you; that is why you have become insane."

Thus Prophet Hud renounced them and their gods and affirmed his dependence on Allah Who had created him. Hud realized that punishment would be incurred on the disbelievers among his people. It is one of the laws of life. Allah punishes the disbelievers, no matter how rich, tyrannical or great they are.

Hud and his people waited for Allah's promise. Then a drought spread throughout the land, for the sky no longer sent its rain. The sun scorched the desert sands, looking like a disk of fire which settled on people's heads.

Prophet Hud's people hastened to him asking: "What is that drought Hud?"

Hud answered: "Allah is angry with you. If you believe in Him, He will accept you and the rain will fall and you will become stronger than you are."

They mocked him and became more obstinate, sarcastic and preserve in their unbelief. The drought increased, the trees turned yellow, and plants died.

A day came when they found the sky full of clouds. Hud's people were glad as they came out of their tents crying: "A cloud, which will give us rain!"

The weather changed suddenly from burning dry and hot to stinging cold with wind that shook everything; trees, plants, tents, men and women. The wind increased day after day and night after night.

Hud's people started to flee. They ran to their tents to hide but the gale became stronger, ripping their tents from their stakes. They hid under cloth covers but the gale became stronger and still and tore away the covers. It slashed clothing and skin. It penetrated the apertures of the body and destroyed it. It hardly touched anything before it was destroyed or killed, its core sucked out to decompose and rot. The storm raged for 8 days and 7 nights.

The violent wind did not stop until the entire region was reduced to ruins and its wicked people destroyed, swallowed by the sands of the desert. Only Hud and his followers remained unharmed. They migrated to another place and lived there in peace, worshipping Allah, their true Lord.

Prophet Salih and the She-Camel
A Wise and Trustworthy Servant

After the destruction of the tribe of Ad, the tribe of Thamud succeeded Ad in power and glory. They also fell to idol-worshipping. As their wealth increased so, too, did their evil ways while their virtue decreased. Like the people of Ad, Tyranny and oppression became prevalent as evil men ruled the land.

So Allah sent unto them His Prophet Salih (peace be upon him), a man from among them. He called his people to worship Allah alone, and to not associate partners with Him. Again, while some of them believed him, the majority of them disbelieved and harmed him by both words and deeds. Prophet Salih was known for his wisdom, purity and goodness and had been greatly respected by his people before Allah's revelation came to him.

Salih's people said to him: "O Salih! You have been among us as a figure of good hope and we wished for you to be our chief, but now you want us to leave our gods and to worship your God (Allah) alone! Do you now forbid us to worship what our fathers worshipped?"

The proof of Salih's message was evident, but despite this it was obvious that most of his people did not believe him. They doubted his words, thinking that he would not stop preaching. They asked him to prove that he was a messenger of Allah by performing a miracle. They said, "Let a unique she (female) camel come from the mountains."

The people of Thamud gathered on a certain day at their meeting place, and prophet Salih came and addressed them to believe in Allah, reminding them of the favors Allah had granted them.

Then pointing at a rock, they demanded: "Ask your Lord to make a she camel, which must be 10 months pregnant, tall and attractive, issue from the rock for us."

Salih replied: "Look now! If Allah sends you what you have requested, just as you have described. Will you believe?"

They answered: "Yes."

So he took a vow from them on this, then prayed to Allah the Almighty to grant their request.

Allah ordered the distant rock to split apart, and a great ten month pregnant she camel came. When their eyes set on it, they were amazed. They saw a great thing, a wonderful sight, a dazzling power and clear evidence!

A number of Salih's people believed, yet most of them continued in their disbelief, stubbornness, and going astray.

The she camel was miraculous because a rock in the mountain split open and it came forth from it, followed by its young offspring. Some said that the she camel used to drink all the water in the wells in one day, and no other animals could approach the water. Some claimed that the she camel produced milk sufficient for all the people to drink, on the same day that it drank all the water, leaving none for them.

At first, the people of Thamud were greatly surprised when the she camel issued from the mountain rocks. It was a blessed camel, and its milk sufficient for thousands of men, women and children. If it slept in a place that place was abandoned by other animals. Thus it was clear this camel was not an ordinary camel, but one of Allah's signs. The she camel lived among Salih's people, some of whom believed in Allah while the majority continued in their obstinacy and disbelief.

Their hatred of Salih turned towards the blessed camel and they became centered on it. A conspiracy started to be hatched against the camel by the disbelievers, and they secretly plotted to harm her. Salih feared that they might kill the camel, so he warned them: "O my people! This she camel of Allah is a sign to you, leave her to feed on Allah's earth, and if you harm her, Allah will punish you."

Salih's people let the camel graze and drink freely, but in their hearts they hated it. However, the miraculous appearance of the unique camel caused many to become Salih's followers, and they clung to their belief in Allah.

The disbelievers now began complaining that this huge she camel with its unusual qualities drank most of the water and frightened their cattle. So they laid a plot to kill the camel, and they sought the help of their women to tempt the men to carry out their commands.

Many women offered their daughters to a young man, Qudar Ibn Saluf, in return for killing the camel. Naturally these young men were tempted and set about to finding seven other men to assist them in killing the camel.

So they watched the camel, observing all its movements. As the she camel came to drink at the well, a young man named Masrai Ibn Mahra shot it in the leg with an arrow. It tried to escape but she was in pain. Qudar followed the camel and struck it with a sword in the other leg. As she fell to the ground, he pierced her with his sword.

The killers were given a hero's welcome, cheered with songs and poetry composed in their praise. In their arrogance they mocked Salih, but he warned them: "Enjoy life for 3 more days then the punishment will descend upon you." Salih was hoping that they would see the folly of their ways and change their attitude before the 3 days went out. "Why 3 days?" they asked. "Let the punishment come as quickly as possible."

He pleaded with them: "My people, why do you hasten to evil rather than good?

Why you do not ask Allah to forgive you so that you may receive mercy?"

Three days after later, thunderbolts filled the air, followed by severe earthquakes which destroyed the entire tribe and its homeland. The land was violently shaken, destroying all living creatures in it. There was one terrific cry which had hardly ended when the disbelievers of Salih's people were struck dead, one and all, at the same time. Neither their strong buildings nor their rock cut homes could protect them.

All were destroyed before they realized what was happening. As for the people who believed in the message of Salih (peace be upon him), they were saved because they had left the place.

Prophet Abraham (Ibrahim)
The Friend of God

Some of the People of the Book stated that when Abraham's father was seventy five years old, he had Abraham, Nahor (Nohour) and Haran. Haran had a son named Lot. They also said that Abraham was the middle child and that Haran died in the lifetime of his father in the land where he was born, the land of Babylonia. At that time people worshipped idols of stone and wood; others worshipped the planets, stars, sun and moon; still others worshipped their kings and rulers.

Abraham was born into that atmosphere, into a typical family of that ancient time. The head of the family was not even an ordinary idolater, but was one who totally rejected God (Allah) and who used to make the idols with his own hands. Some traditions claimed that Abraham's father died before his birth and he was raised by an uncle whom Abraham called father. Other traditions said that his father was alive and was named Azer.

Into that family Abraham was born, destined to stand against his own family, against the entire system of his community. In brief, he stood against all kinds of polytheism. Abraham was endowed with spiritual understanding from an early age. Allah enlightened his heart and mind and gave him wisdom from childhood.

During his early childhood Abraham realized that his father made strange statues. One day, he asked him about what it was he made. His father replied that he made statues of gods.

Abraham was astonished and he spontaneously rejected the idea. Being a child he played with such statues sitting on their backs as people sit on the backs of donkeys and mules.

One day his father saw him riding the statue of Mardukh and he became furious. He ordered his son not to play with it again. Abraham asked: "What is this statue, father? It has big ears, bigger than ours."

His father answered: "It is Mardukh, the god of gods, son! These big ears show his deep knowledge."

This made Abraham laugh, he was only seven years old at that time.

Years passed and Abraham grew. Since his childhood his heart had been full of hatred for these idols. He could not understand how a sane person could make a statue and then worship what he had made. He noticed that these idols did not eat, drink or talk and they could not even turn themselves right side up if someone turned them upside down. How, then could people believe that such statues could harm or benefit them?

Abraham's people had a big temple full of idols, in the middle of which was a niche accommodating the biggest gods which was of different kinds, qualities and shapes. Abraham, who used to go to the temple with his father when he was a child, greatly despised all that wood and stone. What surprised him was the way his people behaved when they entered the temple; they bowed and started to cry, begging and imploring their gods for help as if the idols could hear or understand these requests!

At first, such a sight seemed funny to Abraham, but later he began to feel angry. Was it not astonishing that all those people could be deceived? What added to the problem was that his father wanted him to be a priest when he was grown, but Abraham never stopped displaying his hatred and disdain of them. One night Abraham left his house to go to a mountain. He walked alone in the dark until he chose a cave in the mountain where he sat resting his back against its wall. He looked at the sky. He had hardly seen it when he remembered that he was looking at planets and stars which were worshipped by some people on earth. His young heart was filled with tremendous pain.

He considered what was beyond the moon, the stars and the planets (i.e. Allah) and was astonished that these celestial bodies were worshipped by men when they had been created to worship and obey their Creator, appearing and disappearing at His command.

Therefore Abraham, addressed his people who worshipped celestial bodies. In that debate, Abraham clarified to his people that these celestial bodies do not serve as deities and cannot be worshipped as partners with Allah the Almighty. Indeed these bodies are created things and made to serve humans. They appear sometimes and disappear at others, going out of sight from our world. However, Allah the Almighty does not lose sight of anything, and nothing can be hidden from Him.

Abraham made it clear to them, first that the celestial bodies are unworthy of worship and second that they are among the signs of Allah. Almighty Allah commanded: And from among His Signs are the night and the day, and the sun and the moon. Prostrate not to the sun nor to the moon, but prostrate to Allah Who created them if you really worship Him.

Abraham's reasoning helped to reveal the truth, and then the conflict between him and his people began for the worshippers of the stars and planets did not stand mute. They began arguing and threatening Abraham.

Abraham felt that it was his duty as a good son to advise his father against this evil so that he could be saved from Allah's punishment. Being a wise son he did not make his father feel foolish, nor did he openly laugh at his conduct. He told him that he loved him, thereby hoping to generate fatherly love. Then he gently asked him why he worshipped lifeless idols who could not hear, see or protect him. Before his father could become angry he hastily added: "O my father! Verily! There has come to me of knowledge that which came not unto you. So follow me. I will guide you to a Straight Path. O my father! Worship not Satan. Verily! Stan has been a rebel against the Most Beneficent (Allah).

The father said: "Do you reject my gods, O Abraham? If you stop not this, I will indeed stone you. So get away from me safely before I punish you." Abraham said: "Peace be on you! I will ask Forgiveness of my Lord for you. His father's harsh treatment did not stop Abraham from delivering the message of truth. Abraham left his father's house and abandoned his people and what they worshipped. He decide to do something about their state of disbelief, but did not reveal it. He knew that there was going to be a great celebration on the other bank of the river which would be attended by all the people.

Abraham waited until the city was empty, then came out cautiously, directing his steps towards the temple. The streets leading to it were empty and the temple itself was deserted for the priests had also gone to the festival outside the city.

Abraham went there carrying a sharp axe. He looked at the stone and wood statues of the gods and at the food laid in front of them as offerings. He approached one of the statues and asked: "The food in front of you is getting cold. Why don't you eat?" the statue kept silent and rigid. Abraham asked all the other statues around him: "Will you not eat of the offering before you?"

He was mocking them for he knew they would not eat. He once again asked then: "What is the matter with you that you do not speak?"

Abraham then raised his axe and started smashing the false gods worshipped by the people. He destroyed them all except one on whose neck he hung the axe. After this his anger subsides and he felt at peace. He left the temple. He had fulfilled his vow to show his people a practical proof of their foolishness in worshipping something other than Allah. When the people returned, they were shocked to see their gods smashed to pieces, lying scattered all over the temple. They began to guess who had done that to their idols and Abraham's name came to their minds.

Furious, they demanded that Abraham be arrested and tried. Abraham did not resist. This was precisely what he had been aiming for, so that he could show them up in public for their foolish beliefs.

At the trial they asked him if he was responsible for breaking the idols. Smiling, he told them to ask the biggest idol which was still whole. He told them that he must be the culprit! They replied that he knew well that the idol could not speak or move which gave Abraham the chance to prove the foolishness of worshipping these lifeless objects.

They then realized the senselessness of their beliefs; however, their arrogance would not allow them to admit their foolishness. All they could do was to use their power of authority as tyrants usually do to punish Abraham. They kept him in chains and planned their revenge.

Anger was burning in their hearts. They decided to throw Abraham into the biggest fire they could build. All the citizens were ordered to gather wood as a service to their gods. Ignorant, sick women vowed that if they were cured they would donate so much wood to burn Abraham. For several days they collected fuel.

They dug a deep pit, filled it with firewood and ignited it. They brought a catapult with which to cast Abraham into the fire. Abraham was put on the catapult, his hands and feet were tied. The fire was ready with its flame reaching the sky. The people stood away from the pit because of the great heat. Then the chief priest gave his order to cast Abraham into the fire.

The angel Gabriel came near Abraham's head and asked him: "O Abraham do you wish for anything?" Abraham replied: "Nothing from you."

The catapult was shot and Abraham was cast into the fire. But his descent into the blaze was as descent on steps in a cool garden. The flames were still there, but they did not burn for Allah the Almighty had issued His command: "O fire! Be you coolness and safety for Abraham."

The fire submitted to the will of Allah, becoming cool and safe for Abraham. It only burned his bonds, and he sat in the midst of the fire as if he were sitting in a garden. He glorified and praised Allah the Almighty, with a heart that contained only his love for Allah. There was not any vacant space therein for fear, awe, or worry. It was filled with love only.

The throng, the chiefs, and the priests sad watching the fire from a distance. It was burning their faces and nearly suffocating them. It kept burning for such a long time that the disbelievers thought it would never be extinguished. When it did burn out, they were greatly amazed to find Abraham coming out of the pit untouched by the fire. Their faces were black from the smoke, but his was bright with the light and grace of Allah. The raging fire had become cool for Abraham and had only charred the ropes which held him. He walked out of the fire as if he were walking out of a garden. Cries of astonishment were heard from the heathens. They wanted to harm him, but Allah made them the worst losers.

This miracle shamed the tyrants, but it did not cool the flame of anger in their hearts. However after this event many of the people followed Abraham, although some kept their belief a secret for fear of harm or death at the hands of the rulers. Abraham had established a definite reasoning against idolaters. Nothing was left for him except to reason against the people who proclaimed themselves gods.

When the king, Namrud, heard of Abraham's safe exit from the fire he became very angry. He feared that the status of godhead he had proclaimed for himself was not challenged by an ordinary human being. He summoned Abraham to the palace and held a dialogue with him.

Abraham said to him: "My Lord (Allah) is He Who gives life and causes death." Namrud said: "I give life and cause death." Abraham said: "Allah causes the sun to rise from the east; then cause it you to rise from the west." But Namrud could not and was utterly defeated.

Abraham's fame spread throughout the entire kingdom. People talked about how he had been saved from the blazing fire and how he had debated with the king and left him speechless. In the meantime, Abraham continued calling people to believe in God, exerting a great effort to guide his people to the right path. He tried every means to convince them. However in spite of his love and care for his people, they felt angry and deserted him. Only one woman and one man of his people shared his belief in Allah. The woman's name was Sarah and she became his wife. The man's name was Lot and he became a prophet.

When Abraham realized that no one else was going to believe in his call, he decided to emigrate. He left his people and traveled with his wife and Lot to a city called Ur, then another called Haran, and then to Palestine. After Palestine, Abraham traveled to Egypt, calling people to believe in Allah wherever he traveled, judging fairly between people, and guiding them to truth and righteousness.

Abraham's wife Sarah was sterile. She had been given an Egyptian woman Hajar, as a servant. Abraham had aged and his hair was gray and after many years spent in calling people to Allah. Sarah thought she and Abraham were lonely because she could not have a child. Therefore, she offered her husband her servant Hajar in marriage. Hajar gave birth to her first son Ishmael (Ismail) when Abraham was an old man.

The story continues next with Prophet Ismail/Ishmael (peace be upon him).

Prophet Ishmael (Ismail)
Truthful in his promise

One day, Abraham woke up and asked his wife Hajar to get her son and prepare for a long journey. In a few days Abraham started out with his wife Hajar and their son Ishmael. The child was still nursing and not yet weaned. Abraham walked through cultivated land, desert, and mountains until he reached the desert of the Arabian Peninsula and came to an uncultivated valley having no fruit, no trees, no food, and no water. The valley had no sign of life. After Abraham had helped his wife and child to dismount, he left them with a small amount of food and water which was hardly enough for 2 days. He turned around and walked away. He wife hurried after him asking: "Where are you going Abraham, leaving us in this barren valley?"

Abraham did not answer her, but continued walking. She repeated what she had said, but he remained silent. Finally she understood that he was not acting on his own initiative. She realized that Allah had commanded him to do this. She asked him: "Did Allah command you to do so?" He replied: "Yes." Then his great wife said: "We are not going to be lost, since Allah Who has commanded you is with us."

Abraham brought his wife and his son Ishmael to a place near the Kaba (Mecca) under a tree on the spot of ZamZam water. During those days there was nobody in Mecca, nor was there any water so he made them sit over there and placed near them a leather bag containing some dates and a small water skin containing some water and set out homeward.

Ishmael's mother went on suckling Ishmael and drinking from the water (she had). When the water in the water skin had been used up, she became thirsty and her child also became thirsty, she started looking at Ishmael tossing in agony. She left him, for she could not endure looking at him, and found that the mountain of As-Safa was the nearest mountain to her on that land. She started looking at the valley keenly so that she might see somebody, but she could not see anybody. Then she descended for As-Safa and when she reached the valley, she tucked up her robe and ran in the valley like a person in distress and trouble till she crossed the valley and reached the mountain of Al-Marwa. There she stood and started looking expecting to see somebody, but she could not see anybody. She repeated that running between Safa and Marwa seven times.

The prophet Muhammad (peace be upon him) said: "This is the source of the tradition of the Sa'y (rituals of the hajj, pilgrimage) the going of people between them (As-Safa and Al-Marwa). When she reached Al Marwa (for the last time) she heard a voice and she asked herself to be quiet and listened attentively. She heard the voice again and said: "O whoever you maybe! You have made me hear your voice; have you got something to help me?" And behold! She saw an angel at the place of ZamZam, digging the earth with his heel (or his wing) till water flowed from that place. She started to make something like a basin around it, using her hand in this way, and started filling her water skin with water with her hands."

The angel said to her: "Don't be afraid of being neglected, for this is the House of Allah which will be built by this boy and his father, and Allah never neglects His people."

She lived in that way till some people from the tribe of Jurhum or a family from Jurhum passed by her. Ishmael's mother was sitting near the water. They asked her: "Do you allow us to stay with you?" She replied: "Yes, but you will have no right to possess the water." They agreed to that. Ishmael's mother was pleased with the whole situation, as she used to love to enjoy the company of the people, so they settled there, and later on they sent for their families who came and settled with them so that some families became permanent residents there.

One day Abraham said: "O my son! I have seen in a dream that I am slaughtering you (offer you in sacrifice to Allah), so look what do you think! "O my father! Do that which you are commanded InshAllah (if Allah wills), you shall find me of the patient."

Then when they had both submitted themselves to the Will of Allah and he had laid him for slaughtering, Allah called out to him: "O Abraham! You have fulfilled the dream." Then Allah gave him a great ram to sacrifice instead. This is how Allah rewards the good people.

One day when Abraham came to visit, he saw Ishmael under a tree near ZamZam, sharpening his arrows. When he saw Abraham, he rose up to welcome him. Abraham said: 'O Ishmael! Allah has given me an order.' Ishmael said: 'Do what your Lord has ordered you to do.' Abraham asked: 'Will you help me?' Ishmael said: 'I will help you.' Abraham said: 'Allah has ordered me to build a house here,' pointing to a hillock higher than the land surrounding it.

Ishmael brought the stones while Abraham built and when the walls became high Ishmael brought this stone and put it for Abraham who stood over it and carried on building.

While Ishmael was handing him the stones, and both of them were saying: "Our Lord! Accept this service from us." The Prophet (peace be upon him) added: "Then both of them went on building and going round the Kaba saying O our Lord! Accept this service from us, You are the All Hearer, the All Knower."

Time passed. One day Abraham was sitting outside his tent thinking of his son Ishmael and Allah's sacrifice. His heart was filled with awe and love for Allah for His countless blessings. A big tear dropped from his eyes and reminded him of Ishmael.

In the meantime, three angels descended to the earth; Gabriel, Israphael, and Michael. They came in human shapes and saluted Abraham. Abraham arose and welcomed them. He took them inside his tent thinking they were strangers and guests. He seated them and made sure that they were comfortable, then excused himself to go to his people.

His wife Sarah arose when he entered. She had become old and white haired. Abraham said to her: "We have three strangers in the house." "Who are they?" she asked. "I do not know any of them," he answered. "What food have we got?" He asked. Half a sheep." she replied, "Half a sheep! Slaughter a fat calf for them; they are strangers and guests."

The servants roasted and served a calf. Abraham invited the angels to eat and he started eating so as to encourage them. He continued, but when he glanced at his guests, he noticed that none of them had touched the food. He said to them: "Are you not going to eat?" He resumed eating, but when he glanced at them again he found that they were still not eating. Their hands did not reach out for the food. Abraham began to fear them.

Abraham's fears increased. The angels, however were reading his inner thoughts and one of them said: "Do not fear. We do not eat. We are Allah's angels." One of them then turned towards his wife and conveyed the glad tidings about son Isaac (Ishaaq), and after him grandson Jacob.

Prophet Lot (Lut)

A Righteous and Wise Servant

Prophet Abraham (peace be upon him) left Egypt accompanied by his nephew Lot (peace be upon him), who then went to the city of Sodom, which was on the western shore of the Dead Sea.

This city was filled with evil. Its residents robbed and killed travelers. Another common thing among them was that men married other men instead of women. It was at the height of these crimes and sins that Allah revealed to Prophet Lot (peace upon him) that he should summon the people to talk to them about God, but they were so deeply sunk in their immoral habits that they were deaf to Lot's preaching. Swamped in their unnatural desires, they refused to listen, even when Lot warned them of Allah's punishment. Instead, they threatened to drive him out of the city if he kept on preaching.

The doings of Lot's people saddened his heart. As the years passed, he persisted in his mission but to no avail. No one responded to his call and believed except for the members of his family, and even in his household, not all the members believed. Lot's own wife, like Noah's wife, was a disbeliever. If home is the place of comfort and rest, then Lot found none, for he was tormented both inside and outside his home. His life was continuous torture and he suffered greatly, but he remained patient and steadfast with his people.

The years rolled by, and still not one believed in him. Instead, they belittled his message and mockingly challenged him: "Bring Allah's Torment upon us if you are one of the truthful!"

Overwhelmed with despair, Lot prayed to Allah to grant him victory and destroy the corrupt. Therefore, the angels left Abraham (peace be upon him) and headed for Sodom the town of Lut. They reached the walls of the town in the afternoon. The first person who caught sight of them was Lot's daughter, who was sitting beside the river, filling her jug with water. When she lifted her face and saw them, she was stunned that there could be men of such magnificent beauty on earth.

One of the tree men (angels) asked her: "O maiden, is there a place to rest?"

Remembering the character of her people she replied, "Stay here and do not enter until I inform my father and return." Leaving her jug by the river, she swiftly ran home.

"O father!" she cried. "You are wanted by young men at the town gate and I have never before seen the like of their faces!"

Lot felt distressed as he quickly ran to his guests. He asked them where they came from and where they were going. They did not answer his questions. Instead they asked if he could host them. He started talking with them and impressed upon them the subject of his people's nature.

Lot was filled with turmoil; he wanted to convince his guests without offending them, not to spend the night there, yet at the same time he wanted to extend to them the expected hospitality normally accorded to guests. In vain he tried to make them understand the perilous situation. At last, therefore, he requested them to wait until the night fell, for then no one would see them.

When darkness fell on the town, Lot escorted his guest to his home. No one was aware of their presence. However, as soon as Lot's wife saw them, she slipped out of the house quietly so that no one noticed her. Quickly, she ran to her people with the news and it spread to all the inhabitants like wildfire. The people rushed towards Lot quickly and excitedly. Lot was surprised by their discovery of his guests, and he wondered who could have informed them. The matter became clear, however, when he could not find his wife, anywhere, thus adding grief to his sorrow.

When Lot saw the mob approaching his house, he shut the door, but they kept on banging on it. He pleaded with them to leave the visitors alone and fear Allah's punishment. He urged them to go to their wives.

Lot's people waited until he had finished his short sermon, and then they roared with laughter. Then they broke down the door. Lot became very angry, but he stood powerless before these violent people. He was unable to prevent the abuse of his guests, but he firmly stood his ground and continued to plead with the mob.

At that terrible moment, he wished he had the power to push them away from his guests. Seeing him in a state of helplessness, and grief the guests said: "Do not be anxious or frightened, Lot for we are angels, and these people will not harm you."

On hearing this, the mob was terrified and fled from Lot's house, hurling threats at him as they left. The angels warned Prophet Lot (peace be upon him) to leave his house before sunrise, taking with him all his family except his wife.

Allah had decreed that the city of Sodom should perish. An earthquake rocked the town. It was as if a mighty power had lifted the entire city and flung it down in one jolt. A storm of stones rained on the city. Everyone and everything was destroyed, including Lot's wife.

The book was closed on the people of Lot (peace be upon him). Their towns and names have been erased from the face of the earth. Gone are they from memory.

Lot proceeded towards Abraham (peace be upon them). He visited him, and when he recounted the story of his people, he was surprised to learn that Abraham already knew. So Lot continued to invite people to Allah, as did Abraham, and the two held firm to their mission.

Prophets Isaac (Ishaq) and Yaqub/Jacob
Righteous Sons Heralded by the Angels

When Abraham felt that his life was drawing to a close, he wished to see Isaac married. He did not want Isaac to marry one of the Canaanites, who were pagans, so he sent a trustworthy servant to Haran in Iraq to choose a bride for Isaac. The servant's choice fell upon Rebekah who was a daughter of Abraham's brother. Isaac married her and she gave birth to a set of twins, Esau (Al Eis) and Jacob (Yaqub), which means Israel, (belonging to the people of Israel).

Bad feelings developed between the two brothers when they grew into manhood. Esau disliked the fact that Jacob was favored by his father and by Allah with prophethood. This bad feeling became so serious that Esau threatened to kill his brother. Fearing for his life, Jacob fled the country.

When their mother knew that Esau threatened his brother Jacob, she commanded her son Jacob to go to her brother Laban in the land of Haran and abide with him for a time until his brother's anger had abated, and to marry one of the Laban's daughters.

Jacob (peace be upon him) left his family, when night came he found a place to rest. He took a stone and put it under his head and slept. He dreamed of a ladder from heaven to earth. Angels were ascending and descending and the Lord addressed him and said to him; "I will bless you and your offspring and make this land for you and for those who come after you."

When he awoke he felt joyful from what he had seen in his dream and vowed, for Allah's sake that if he returned to his family safely, he would build here a temple for Allah the Almighty. He also vowed to give one tenth of his property for the sake of Allah. He poured oil on the stone so as to recognize it and called the place "Ayle's House" (Bethel), which means "House of Allah". It was to be the location of Jerusalem later.

The People of the Book also said that when Jacob came to his maternal uncle in the land of Haran. His uncle had two daughters. The elder one was called Leah (Lia) and the younger one was Rachel (Rahil). The latter was the better and lovelier of the two. His uncle agreed to marry his daughter to him on the condition that Jacob pasture his sheep for seven years.

After a period of time, his uncle prepared a feast and gathered people for the wedding. He married Leah, his elder daughter, to him at night. She was weak-sighted and ugly. When morning came, Jacob discovered she was Leah and he complained to his uncle. "You deceived me; I was engaged to Rachel and you married me to Leah." His uncle said: "It is not our tradition to marry the younger daughter before the elder daughter. However, if you love her sister, work another seven years and I will marry you to both of them."

Jacob worked for seven years and then married Rachel. It was acceptable in their time, as described in the Torah, for a man to marry two sisters. Laban gave a female slave to each daughter. Leah's slave was called Zilpah and Rachel's slave was called Bilha.

Almighty Allah compensated Leah's weakness by giving her sons. The first one was named Rueben (Robel), after whom there were Simon (Shamun), Levi (Lawi), and Judah (Yahudh). Rachel felt jealous of Leah's having sons, as she was barren. She gave her slave Bilha to her husband and he had relations with her until she became pregnant. She gave birth to a son and named him Naphtali. Leah was vexed that Rachel's slave had given birth to a son, so she in turn gave her slave Zilpah to Jacob (peace be upon him), Zilpah gave birth to two sons, Gad and Asher. Then Leah got pregnant and gave birth to her fifth son, Issaacher, and later she gave birth to a sixth son Zebulun. After this Leah gave birth to a daughter named Dinah. Thus, Leah had seven sons from Jacob.

Then Rachel prayed to Allah to give her a son from Jacob. Allah heard her call and responded to her prayer. She gave birth to a son, great, honorable, and beautiful. She named him Joseph (Yusuf).

All of this happened when they were in the land of Haran and Jacob was pasturing his uncle's sheep, which he did for a period of twenty years. Jacob then asked his uncle Laban to let him go and visit his family. His uncle said to him: "I have been blessed because of you; ask for whatever money you need." Jacob said: "Give me each spotted and speckled goat born this year and each black lamb."

At Laban's command his sons removed their father's goat that were striped, spotted or speckled, and the black lambs, lest others should be born with those traits. They walked for three days with their father's goats and sheep while Jacob tended the remaining flock.

The People of the Book said that Jacob (peace be upon him) took fresh rods of poplar, almond, and plane. He peeled streaks in them and cast them into the water through for the goats to look at. The young inside their abdomens were terrified and moved and they were born striped, spotted or speckled. When the sheep were breeding, he set their faces towards the black sheep in Laban's flock and put the rods among them. Their lambs were born black. This was considered an example of supernatural powers, a miracle. Jacob had many goats, sheep, beast and slaves. His uncle and his sons' faces changed as if they the sheep and goats had been stolen from them.

Allah the Almighty inspired Jacob to return to the country of his father and people, and He promised to stand by him. Jacob told his family that, and they responded and obeyed him. Jacob did not tell Laban of his plans, however, and left without bidding farewell.

Upon leaving, Rachel stole her father's idols. After Jacob and his people had fled for his country, Laban and his people followed them. When Laban met with Jacob, he blamed him for leaving him without his knowledge. He would have liked to know so that he could have made them leave with celebration and joy, with drums and songs, and so that he could have bidden his daughters and sons farewell. And why have they taken his idols with them? Jacob had no knowledge of his idols, so he denied that had taken them from him. Then Laban entered the tents of his daughters and slaves to search, but he found nothing, for Rachel had put the idols in the camel saddle under her. She did not get up, apologizing that she is not feeling well. Thus, he could not perceive what they had done.

Then they sat on a hill called Galeed and made a covenant there. Jacob would not ill-treat Laban's daughters nor marry others. Neither Laban nor Jacob would pass the hill into the other's country. They cooked food and their people ate with them. Each bade the other farewell as they departed, each returning to his own country.

When Jacob approached the land of Seir, the angels greeted him. He sent a messenger ahead with greetings to his brother Esau, asking forgiveness and humbling himself before him. The messenger returned greetings and told Jacob that Esau was riding towards him with four hundred men. This made Jacob afraid and he entreated and prayed to Allah Almighty. He prostrated in humiliation and asked Him to fulfill His promise which He had made before. He asked Him to stop the evil of his brother Esau. Then Jacob prepared a great present for his brother: two hundred female goats and twenty male goats, two hundred ewes and twenty rams, and thirty milch camels, forty cows and two bulls, twenty female donkeys and ten male donkeys.

He commanded his slaves to take the animals, each drove by itself, and pass on ahead of him with a space between the droves. He instructed them: "When you meet my brother Esau he will ask you, 'to whom do you belong? Where are you going?' you shall say, 'they belong to your servant Jacob; they are a present to my master Esau. Moreover, he is behind us."

Jacob stayed behind with his two wives, his slaves and his children for two nights, then continued walking by night and resting by day.

When the dawn of the second day came one of the angels appeared in the shape of a man. Jacob began to wrestle with him. They were neck and neck until the angel injured his thigh and Jacob became lame. When the day was breaking, the angel said to him: 'What is your name?' He answered: 'Jacob.' The angel said: "After today you shall not be called anything but Israel." Jacob asked: "Who are you? What is your name?" He vanished. Then Jacob knew that he was one of the angels. Jacob was lame, and for this reason the children of Israel do not eat the thigh muscle on the hip socket.

Jacob raised his eyes and saw his brother Esau coming. Jacob prostrated seven times before him for it was their salutation in that time. It was lawful for them just as the angels had prostration in salutation to Adam.

When Esau saw him, he ran towards him, embraced and kissed him and wept. When Esau raised his eyes and saw the women and children he asked: "Who are these with you?" Jacob answered: "Those whom Allah has given me, your servant." Leah, Rachel, their slaves, and all the children approached and prostrated before him. Jacob asked Esau to accept his gift and insisted until he did so. Esau returned and went in advance before him. Jacob and his family followed with the flocks and herds and slaves to the mountains (Seir).

When he came to Succoth (Sahur), he built a house for himself and shades for his beasts. Then he passed by Jerusalem, the village of Shechem, and camped before the village. He bought a farm from Shcehm Ibn Hamor with one hundred goats and built an altar, which he called Ayl, as Allah commanded him.

He built the altar where Jerusalem stands today and later Solomon son of David rebuilt it. It is in the place of the stone which he had earlier anointed with oil as was mentioned before.

Rachel got pregnant and gave birth to a son, Benjamin, but she had a hard labor and died after delivery. Jacob buried her in Ephrath (afrath). The tomb of Rachel is there till the present day. Jacob's sons were twelve men. Jacob came to his father Isaac and settled with him in the village of Hebron which lies in the land of Canaan where Abraham had lived. Then Isaac fell ill and died when he was one hundred eighty years old. His sons Esau and Jacob buried him with his father Abraham (peace be upon them) in a cave which he had bought. It was said that Abraham died at the age of one hundred seventy five.

Prophet Joseph (Yusuf)

A Truthful and Forgiving Servant

This is a detailed and fascinating story involving both human weaknesses such as jealousy, hatred, pride, passion, deception, intrigue, cruelty, and terror as well as noble qualities such as patience, loyalty, bravery, nobility, and compassion.

Joseph lived all his life confronting schemes made by the people closest to him. The story begins with a dream and ends with its interpretation. As the sun appeared over the horizon, bathing the earth in its morning glory, Joseph (peace be upon him), son of the Prophet Jacob (peace be upon him) awoke from his sleep, delighted by a pleasant dream he had had. Filled with excitement he ran to his father and related it.

"O my father! I saw (in a dream) eleven stars and the sun and the moon, I saw them prostrating themselves to me."

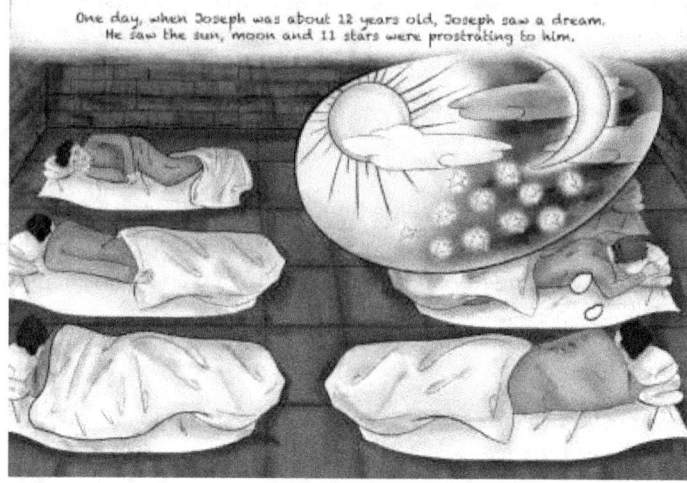

His father's face lit up. He foresaw that Joseph would be one through whom the prophecy of his grandfather, Prophet Abraham (peace be upon him), would be fulfilled, in that his offspring would keep the light of Abraham's house alive and spread Allah's message to mankind. However, the father was well aware of the jealousy of Joseph's brothers, so he warned him against telling his dream to his brothers. "O my son! Relate not your vision to your brothers, lest they arrange a plot against you. Verily! Satan is to man an open enemy!

Joseph heeded his father's warning. He did not tell his brothers what he had seen. It is well known that they hatred him so much that it was difficult for him to feel secure telling them what was in his heart and in his dreams. Joseph was very handsome and robust, with a gentle temperament. He was respectful, kind and considerate. His brother Benjamin was equally pleasant. Both were from one mother, Rachel. Because of their refined qualities, the father loved the two more than his other children, and would not let them out of his sight. To protect them, he kept them busy with work in the house garden.

In spite of this, his brothers sat down to conspire against Joseph. One of them asked: "Why does our father love Joseph more than us?"

Another answered: "Perhaps because of his beauty."

A third said: "Joseph and his brother occupied our father's heart."

The first complained: "Our father has gone all astray."

One of them suggested a solution to the matter; kill Joseph.

"Where should we kill him?"

"We should banish him away from these grounds."

"We will send him to a distant land."

"Why should we not kill him and have rest so that the favor of your father may be given to you alone?"

However, Judah (Yahudh), the eldest and most intelligent among them, said: "There is no need to kill him when all you want is to get rid of him. Look here, let us throw him into a well and he will be picked up by a passing caravan. They will take him with them to a distant land. He will disappear from your father's sight and our purpose will be served with his exile. Then after that we shall repent for our crime and become good people once again."

They said: "O our father! Why do you not trust us with Joseph, when we love him? Send him with us tomorrow to enjoy himself and play, and we will take care of him."

He (Jacob) said: "Truly, it saddens me that you should take him away. I fear lest a wolf should devour him, while you are careless of him."

They said: "If a wolf devours him, while we are a strong group to guard him, then surely we are the losers."

Jacob suggested a point, which had not occurred to them in their discussion: he feared that desert wolves would eat him! The wolves within them, or did he mean the wild wolves? No one but Allah knows. They coaxed their father to send Joseph with them. Jacob agreed under their pressure. They were excited that they could now get rid of Joseph for after this they could stand a better chance of receiving their father's affection. On leaving home, they went directly to the well, as they had planned, on the pretext of drinking water. One of them put his arms around Joseph and held him tightly. Startled by this unusual behavior, Joseph struggled to free himself. More brothers rushed to hold him. One of them removed his shirt.

Some more joined in to lift Joseph up and cast him into the deep well. Joseph's piteous pleas made no difference to their cruel hearts.

Then Allah revealed to Joseph that he was safe and should not fear, for he would meet them again someday to remind them of what they had done. There was water in the well, which buoyed Joseph's body, so he was not harmed. He sat lonely in the water, then clung to a rock ledge overheard and climbed on top of it. His brothers left him in this desolate place.

Then they killed a sheep and soaked Joseph's shirt in its blood. One brother said that they should swear to keep their deed a close secret. All of them took the oath. And they went to their father in the early part of the night weeping.

Jacob was sitting in his house when the sons entered. The darkness of night covering the darkness of their hearts and the darkness of their lies struggling to come out. Jacob wondered aloud: "Why this weeping? Has anything happened to our flock?" They answered crying: "O our father! We went racing with one another, and left Joseph by our belongings and a wolf devoured him. We were surprised after returning from the race that Joseph was in the belly of the wolf."

"The wolf has eaten Joseph!"

"This is Joseph's shirt. We foiled it soiled with blood, and did not find Joseph!"

Deep down in the heart Jacob knew that his beloved son was still alive and that his other sons were lying. He held the blood stained in his hands, spread it out and remarked: "What a merciful wolf! He ate up my beloved son without tearing his shirt!" Their faces turned red when he demanded more information, but each swore by Allah that he was telling the truth. The brokenhearted father burst into tears: "Nay! But your own selves have made up a tale. So for me patience is more fitting. It is Allah Alone whose Help can be sought against that which you assert."

In the dark well Joseph managed to find a stone ledge to hold onto. Around him was total darkness and an eerie silence. Fearful thoughts entered his mind: what would happen to him? Where would he find food? Why had his own brothers turned against him?

Would his father know of his plight? His father's smile flashed before him recalling the love and affection he had always shown him. Joseph began to pray earnestly, pleading to Allah for salvation. Gradually his fear began to subside. His Creator was testing the young man with a great misfortune in order to fill in him a spirit of patience and courage. Joseph, surrendered himself to the will of his Lord.

While the fearful thoughts entered his mind, gradually he heard voices outside the well. A caravan of merchants on its way to Egypt stopped at this famous well for water. A man lowered in his bucket. Joseph was startled by the bucket hurtling down and grabbed hold of it before it could land in the water. As the man began to haul he felt the load unusually heavy, so he peeped into the well. What he saw shocked him; a boy was clinging to the rope! He held the rope tightly and shouted to his friends: "Better give me a hand fellows! Looks like I found real treasure in the well!"

His companions rushed to the well and helped him to pull out the stranger holding onto the rope. Standing before them was a healthy, handsome youth, beaming with an angelic smile. They saw in him a handsome prize, for money was all that mattered to them. Immediately, they clapped iron shackles on his feet and took him along to Egypt, far away from his beloved homeland of Canaan.

All over the Egyptian city the news spread that an unusually handsome, robust young slave was on sale. People gathered by the hundreds at the slave market. Some were spectators, others were bidders. Each one craning his neck to view the handsome specimen.

The auctioneer had a field day as the bidding went wild, each buyer trying to outbid the other. Eventually, the Aziz, the chief minister of Egypt, outbid all the others and took Joseph to his mansion.

Joseph was pleasantly surprised when the chief minister of Egypt ordered his men to remove the heavy shackles from his swollen feet. He was also surprised when he told Joseph not to betray his trust; he would not be ill-treated if he behaved himself. Joseph smiled at his benefactor, thanked him, and promised to be loyal.

Joseph felt at ease, for at last he was sheltered and would be well cared for. He thanked Allah over and over and wondered at the mysterious of life. Not so long ago he had been cast into a deep, dark well with no hope of ever coming out alive. Next he was rescued, then enslaved in iron shackles, and now he was moving freely in a luxurious mansion with enough food to enjoy. However, his heart ached with longing for his parents and brother Benjamin, and he shed tears daily.

Joseph was made the personal attendant of the chief minister's wife. He was obedient and ever-obliging. With his pleasant manners and charming behavior, he won everybody's heart.

Joseph's handsomeness became the talk of the town. People referred to him as the most attractive man they had ever seen and wrote poetry about him. His face carried immaculate beauty. The purity of his inner soul and his heart showed in his face, increasing his beauty. People from afar came to the city to have a glimpse of him.

The days passed and Joseph grew. His master soon knew that Allah had graced him with Joseph. He understood that Joseph was the most honest, straightforward and noble person he had met in his life. Therefore, he put Joseph in charge of his household, honored him, and treated him as a son. However, the wife of the chief minister, Zulaikha, watched Joseph from day to day. She ate with him, talked with him, listened to him, and her wonder increased over the passion of time.

Joseph was soon confronted (with his second trial). The chief minister's wife, Zulaikha could not resist the handsome Joseph, and her obsession with him caused her sleepless nights. She fell in love with him, and it was painful for her to be so close to a man, yet be unable to hold him. Yet, she was not a bad woman, for in her position she could get any man she desired. She was a very pretty and intelligent lady, or why would the chief minister have chosen her of all the pretty women in the kingdom? Although she bore him no child, he would not take another wife, as he loved her passionately.

One day, Joseph's refusal only heightened her passion. As he moved to the door to escape, she ran after him and caught hold of his shirt, like a drowning person clinging to the boat. In her tugging she tore his shirt and held the torn piece in her hand. They reached the door together. It opened suddenly, there stood her husband and a relative of hers. As he opened the door, he saw her husband standing in front of him. The sly woman immediately changed her tone to anger, and, showing the torn piece of the shirt in her hand, asked her husband: "What is the recompense (punishment) for him who intended an evil design against your wife, except that he be put in prison or a painful torment?"

She was now accusing Joseph of molesting her, to give the impression that she was innocent and a victim of Joseph's desire. Though bewildered Joseph denied it.

The shirt was passed from hand to hand, while she watched. The witness (her cousin) looked at it and found that it was torn at the back. The evidence showed that she was guilty. The disappointed husband remarked to his wife: "Surely, it is a plot of you women!

The wise and just Aziz apologized to Joseph. He also instructed his wife to beg Joseph's forgiveness for accusing him falsely. However, an incident like this cannot remain a secret in a house filled with servants, and the story spread. Women began to see her behavior as scandalous.

Naturally their gossip distressed Zulaikha. She honestly believed that it was not easy for any women to resist a man as handsome as Joseph. To prove her helplessness, she planned to subject the women to the same temptation she faced. She invited them to a lavish banquet. No one so invited would want to miss the honor of dining with the chief minister's wife; besides, they secretly harbored the desire to meet the handsome Joseph face to face. Some of her close friends jokingly said they would come only if she introduced them to Joseph. The invitation was restricted to ladies. The banquet began, laughter and mirth abounded.

Etiquette dictated that the ladies not mention the topic of Joseph. They were shocked, therefore, when Zulaikha opened the topic. "I have heard of those who say I have fallen in love with the young Hebrew man, Joseph."

Silence fell upon the banquet. At once all the guests hands stopped, and all eyes fell on the chief minister's wife. She said, while giving orders for the fruit to be served: "I admit that he is charming fellow. I do not deny that I love him. I have loved him for a long time."

The confession of the chief minister's wife removed the tension among the ladies. After finishing their dinner, the guests began cutting their fruit. At that very moment she summoned Joseph to make his appearance. He entered the hall gracefully, his gaze lowered. Zulaikha called him by his name and he raised his head. The guests were astonished and dumbfounded. His face was shining and beautiful. It reflected complete innocence, so much so that one could feel the peace of mind in the depth of his soul.

They exclaimed in astonishment while continuing to cut the fruit. All their eyes were on Joseph. So it was that the women began to cut their hands without feeling that they had cut them. One of the ladies gasped: "Good gracious!" Another whispered: "This is not a mortal being!" Another stammered, patting her hair: "This is but a noble angel."

Then the chief minister's wife stood up and announced: "This is the one for whom I have been blamed. I do not deny that I tempted him. You have been enchanted by Joseph, and see what has happened to your hands. I have tempted him, and if he does not do what I want of him he shall be imprisoned."

That evening, Zulaikha convinced her husband that the only way to save her honor was to put Joseph in prison; otherwise she would not be able to control herself or to safeguard his prestige. The chief minister knew Joseph was absolutely innocent, that he was a young man of honor, a loyal servant, and he loved him for these reasons. It was not an easy decision for him to put an innocent man behind bars. However, he was left with no choice. He reasoned that Joseph's honor would also be safeguarded if he was kept out of Zulaikha's sight. That night, with a heavy heart, the chief minister sent Joseph to prison.

Prison was Joseph's third test. During this period Allah blessed him with an extraordinary gift; the ability to interpret dreams. At about the same time two other men landed in the prison. One was the cupbearer of the king; the other was the king's cook. The two men sensed that Joseph was not a common criminal, for an aura of piety glowed on his face. Both men had vivid dreams, and they were anxious to have them explained. The king's cook dreamed that he stood in a place with bread on his head, and two birds were eating the bread. The cupbearer dreamed that he was serving the king wine. The two went to Joseph and told him their dreams, asking him to give them their meaning. First, Joseph called them to Allah. Then he said that the cook would be crucified until he died and that the cupbearer would return to the service of the king. Joseph told the cupbearer to remember him to the king and to say that there was a wronged soul called Joseph in prison. What Joseph predicted did happen; the cook was crucified and the cupbearer returned to the palace.

After the cupbearer returned to service, Satan made him forget to mention Joseph's name to the king. Therefore, Joseph remained in prison for a few years, but he made patience his own, praying to Allah.

One day, the king was asleep. He saw himself on the banks of the Nile River. The water is receding before him, becoming mere mud. The fish begin to skip and jump in the mud. Seven fat cows come out of the river followed by seven lean cows. The seven lean ones devour the seven fat ones. The king is terrified. The seven ears of green grain grow on the riverbanks and disappear in the mud. One the same spot grow seven dray ears of grain.

The king awoke frightened, shocked, and depressed, not knowing what all this meant. He sent for the sorcerers, priests and ministers, and told them his dream.

The sorcerers said: "This is a mixed up dream. How can any of that be? It is a nightmare."

The priests said: "Perhaps his majesty had a heavy supper."

The chief minister said: "Could it be that his majesty was exposed and did not draw the blanket up at night?" The king's jester said, jokingly: "His majesty is beginning to grow old, and so his dreams are confused."

They reached a unanimous conclusion that it was only a nightmare. The news reached the cupbearer. He recollected the dream he had in prison and compared it to the king's dream, and, therefore Joseph came to mind. He ran to the king to tell him about Joseph, who was the only one capable to interpreting the dream. The cupbearer said: "He had asked me to remember him to you, but I forgot." The king sent the cupbearer to ask Joseph about the dream.

Joseph interpreted it to him: "There will be seven years of abundance. If the land is properly cultivated, there will be an excess of good harvest, more than the people will need. This should be stored. Thereafter, seven years of famine will follow, during which time the excess grain could be used."

He also advised that during the famine they should save some grain to be used for seed for the next harvest. Joseph then added; "After seven years of drought, there will be a year during which water will be plentiful. If the water is properly used, grapevines and olive trees will grow in abundance, providing plenty of grapes and olive oil."

The cupbearer hurried back with the good news. The king was fascinated by Joseph's interpretation. The king was greatly astonished. Who could this person be? He commanded that Joseph be set free from prison and presented to him at once. The king's envoy went to fetch him immediately, but Joseph refused to leave the prison unless his innocence was proven. Perhaps they accused him of cutting the ladies hands, or trying to rape them. Perhaps any other false accusation was made.

We do not know exactly what was said to the people to justify Joseph's sentence to prison. The envoy returned to the king. The king asked him: "Where is Joseph? Did I not command you to fetch him?"

The envoy replied: "He refused to leave until his innocence is established regarding the ladies who cut their hands."

The king ordered: "Bring the wives of the ministers and the wife of the chief minister at once." The king felt that Joseph had been harmed unfairly but he did not know exactly how. The wife of the chief minister came with the other ministers' wives. The king asked: "What is the story of Joseph? What do you know about him? Is it true that...?"

One of the ladies interrupted the king exclaiming: "Allah forbid!"

A second said: "We know of no evil he has done."

A third said: "He enjoys the innocence of angels."

The eyes of everyone turned to the wife of the chief minister. She now wore a wrinkled face and had lost weight. She had been overwhelmed by sorrow over Joseph while he was in prison. She boldly confessed that she had lied and he had told the truth. "I tempted him; but he refused."

She confirmed what she said, not out of fear of the king or the other ladies, but for Joseph to know that she had never betrayed him during his absence, for he was still in her mind and soul. Of all creation he was the only one she cared for, so she confirmed his innocence before all.

We do not know what happened to her after she gave her clear evidence. Yet still, there are legends about her. It has been said that after her husband died she married Joseph. Other legends said that she lost her sight, weeping for Joseph. She abandoned her palace and wandered in the streets of the city.

The king informed Joseph that his innocence was established and ordered him to come to the palace for an interview. The king recognized his noble qualities. When Joseph came, the king spoke to him in his tongue. Joseph's replies astonished the king with his cultural refinement and wide knowledge. Then the conversation turned to the dream. Joseph advised the king to start planning for years of famine ahead. He informed him that the famine would affect not only Egypt but the neighboring countries as well. The king offered him a high position.

Joseph asked to be made controller of the granaries, so that he could guard the nation's harvest and thereby safeguard it during the anticipated drought. By this Joseph did not mean to seize an opportunity or personal gain; he merely wanted to rescue hungry nations for a personal gain; he merely wanted to rescue hungry nations for a period of seven years. It was a sheer self-sacrifice on his part.

The wheels of time turned. During the seven good years, Joseph had full control over the cultivation, harvesting, and storage of crops. During the following seven years, drought followed and famine spread throughout the region, including Canaan, the homeland of Joseph. Joseph advised the king that as his kingdom was blessed with reserved grain, he should sell his grain to the needy nations at a fair price. The king agreed, and the good news spread all over the region.

Jacob sent ten of his sons, all except Benjamin, to Egypt to purchase provisions. Joseph heard of the ten brothers who had come from afar and who could not speak the language of the Egyptians.

When they called on him to purchase their needs, Joseph immediately recognized his brothers, but they did not know him. How could they? To them Joseph no longer existed; he had been thrown into the deep, dark well many years ago!

Joseph received them warmly. After supplying them with provisions, he asked where they had come from. They explained: "We are eleven brothers, the children of a noble prophet. The youngest is at home tending to the needs of our aging father."

On hearing this, Joseph's eyes filled with tears; his longing for home swelled up in his heart, as well as his longing for his beloved parents and his loving brother Benjamin. "Are you truthful people?" Joseph asked them.

Perturbed they replied, "What reason should we have to sate an untruth?"

"If what you say is true then bring your brother as proof and I will reward you with double rations. But if you do not bring him to me, it would be better if you do not return," Joseph warned them. They assured him that they would gladly fulfill his command but that they would have to get their father's permission. As an inducement to return with their brother, Joseph ordered his servant to secretly place the purse, with the money they had paid, into one of their grain sacks.

The scene dims in Egypt and lights in Canaan. The brothers returned to their father. Before they could unload the camels, they greeted him, then reproved him: "We were denied some supplies because you did not let your son go with us. They would not give us food for absentees. Why would you not entrust him with us? Please, send him with us, and we shall take care of him."

Jacob became sad and told them: "I will not permit Benjamin to travel with you. I will not part with him, for I entrusted Joseph to you and you failed me."

Later, when they opened their grain sacks, they were surprised to find the money purse returned intact. They rushed to their father; "Look, father! The noble official has returned our money; this is surely proof that he would not harm our brother and it can only benefit us." But Jacob refused to send Benjamin with them.

After some time, when they had no more grain, Jacob asked them to travel to Egypt for more. They reminded him of the warning the Egyptian official had given them. They could not return without Benjamin. Jacob agreed, but not before he extracted a pledge from them. "I will not send him with you unless you give me a pledge in Allah's name that you shall bring him back to me as safely as you take him." They gave their solemn pledge. He reminded them: "Allah is witness to your pledge." He then advised them to enter the city through several different gates. Jacob blessed them on their departure and prayed to Allah for their protection. The brothers undertook the long journey to Egypt, taking good care of Benjamin.

Joseph welcomed them heartily, although, with difficulty, he suppressed the desire to embrace Benjamin that arose within him. He prepared a feast for them and seated them in pairs. Joseph arranged to sit next to his beloved brother Benjamin, who began to weep. Joseph asked him why he was crying. He replied: "If my brother Joseph had been here, I would have sat next to him."

That night, when Joseph and Benjamin were alone in a room, Joseph asked whether he would have him for a brother. Benjamin respectfully answered that he regarded his host as a wonderful person, but he could never take the place of his brother. Joseph broke down, and amidst flowing tears said; "My loving brother, I am the brother who was lost and whose name you are constantly repeating. Fate has brought us together after many years of separation. This is Allah's favor. But let it be a secret between us for the time being." Benjamin flung his arms around Joseph and both brothers shed tears of joy.

The next day, while their bags were being filled with grains to load onto the camels, Joseph ordered one of his attendants to place the king's gold cup which was used for measuring the grain into Benjamin's saddlebag. When the brothers were ready to set out, the gates were locked, and the court crier shouted: "O you travelers, you are thieves!" The accusation was most unusual, and the people gathered around Joseph's brothers.

"What have you lost?" his brothers inquired.

A soldier said: "The king's golden cup. Whoever can trace it we will give a beast load of grain."

Joseph's brothers said with all innocence: "We have not come here to corrupt the land and steal."

Joseph's officers said (as he had instructed them): What punishment should you choose for the thief?" The brothers answered: "According to our law, whoever steals becomes a slave to the owner of the property."

The officers agreed: "We shall apply your law instead of the Egyptian law, which provides for imprisonment."

The chief officer ordered his soldiers to start searching the caravan. Joseph was watching the incident from high upon his throne. He had given instructions for Benjamin's bag to be the last to be searched.

When they did not find the cup in the bags of the ten older brothers, the brothers sighed in relief. There remained only the bag of their youngest brother. Joseph said, intervening for the first time, that there was no need to search his saddle as he did not look like a thief.

His brothers affirmed: "We will not move an inch unless his saddle is searched as well. We are the sons of a noble man, not thieves."

The soldiers reached in their hands and pulled out the king's cup. The brothers exclaimed: "If he steals now, a brother of his has stolen before." They strayed from the present issue in order to blame a particular group of the children of Jacob.

Joseph heard their resentment with his own ears and was filled with regret. Yet, he swallowed his own resentment, keeping it within. He said to himself, "you went further and fared worse; it shall go bad with you and worse hereafter, and Allah knows your intention."

Silence fell upon them after these remarks by the brothers. Then they forgot their secret satisfaction and thought of Jacob; they had taken an oath with him that they would not betray his son. They began to beg Joseph for mercy. "Joseph, O minister! Take one of us instead. He is the son of a good man, and we can see you are a good man."

Joseph answered calmly: "How can you want to set free the man who has stolen the king's cup? It would be sinful."

The brothers went on pleading for mercy. However, the guards said that the king had spoken and his word was law. Judah, the eldest, was much worried and told the others: "We promised our father in the name of Allah not to fail him. I will, therefore, stay behind and will only return if my father permits me to do so."

They said: "O ruler of the land! Verily, he has an old father who will grieve for him, so take one of us in his place. Indeed we think that you are one of the good doers."

He said: "Allah forbid! That we should take anyone but him with whom we found our property. Indeed if we did so, we shall be Zalimun (wrongdoers)."

The brothers left enough provisions behind for Judah, who stayed at a tavern awaiting the fate of Benjamin. In the meantime, Joseph kept Benjamin in his house as his personal guest and told him how he had devised the plot to put the king's cup in his bag, in order to keep him behind, so as to protect him. He was also glad that Judah had stayed behind, as he was a good hearted brother. Joseph secretly arranged to watch over Judah's wellbeing.

Joseph's plan in sending the others back was to test their sincerity, to see if they would come back for the two brothers they had left behind. When they arrived home, they entered upon their father calling: "O our father! Your son has stolen!"

He was puzzled, scarcely believing the news. He was overwhelmed with sorrow and his eyes wept tears. "Patience be with me; perhaps Allah will return all of them to me. He is Most Knowing, Most Wise." A pal of lonesomeness closed over him, yet he found consolation in patience and trusted in Allah.

The father was deeply hurt. Only prayer could comfort him and strengthen his faith and patience. Weeping all those years for his beloved son Joseph - and now one more of his best sons had been snatched from him - Jacob almost lost his sight.

The other sons pleaded with him: "O father, you are a noble prophet and a great messenger of Allah. Unto you descended revelation and people received guidance and faith from you. Why are you destroying yourself in this way?"

Jacob replied: "Rebuking me will not lessen my grief. Only the return of my sons will comfort me. My sons, go in search of Joseph and his brother; do not despair of Allah's mercy."

Allah, the Almighty told us: They said: "By Allah! You will never cease remembering Joseph until you become weak with old age, or until you be of the dead."

He said: "I only complain of my grief and sorrow to Allah, and I know from Allah that which you know not.

O my sons! Go you and inquire about Joseph and his brother and never give up hope of Allah's Mercy. Certainly no one despairs of Allah's Mercy, except the people who disbelieve."

The caravan set out for Egypt. The brothers - on their way to see the chief minister (Joseph) - were poor and depressed.

On reaching Egypt they collected Judah and called on Joseph, to whom they pleaded: "O ruler of the land! A hard time has hit us and our family, and we have brought but poor capital, so pay us full measure and be charitable to us. Truly, Allah does reward the charitable."

At the end, they begged Joseph. They asked alms of him, appealing to his heart, reminding him that Allah rewards alms givers. At this moment, in the midst of their plight, Joseph spoke to them in their native tongue saying: "Do you know what you did with Joseph and his brother when you were ignorant?" They said: "Are you indeed Joseph?"

He said: "I am Joseph, and his is my brother (Benjamin). Allah has indeed been Gracious to us. Verily, he who fears Allah with obedience to Him (by abstaining from sins and evil deeds, and by performing righteous good deeds), and is patient, then surely, Allah makes not the reward of the good doers to be lost."

They said: "By Allah! Indeed Allah has preferred you above us, and we certainly have been sinners."

The brothers began to tremble with fear, but Joseph comforted them: "No reproach on you this day, may Allah forgive you, and He is the Most Merciful of those who show mercy!"

Joseph embraced them, and together they wept with joy. It was not possible for Joseph to leave his responsible office without proper replacement, so he advised his brothers: "Go with this shirt of mine, and cast it over the face of my father, he will become clear-sighted, and bring to me all your family."

And so the caravan headed back for Palestine. We leave the scene in Egypt and return to Palestine and the house of Jacob. The old man is sitting in his room; tears have been flowing down his cheeks. He stands up all of a sudden, dresses and goes out to his son's wives. Then he lifts up his face to Heaven and sniffs the air.

The wife of the eldest son remarked: "Jacob has come out of his room today." The women inquired about what was amiss. There was a hint of a smile on his face. The others asked him: "How do you feel today?"

He answered: "I can smell Joseph in the air."

The wives left him alone, saying to one another that there was no hope for the old man. 'He will die of weeping over Joseph.'

"Did he talk about Joseph's shirt?"

"I do not know. He said he could smell him; perhaps he has gone mad."

That day the old man wanted a cup of milk to break his fast, for he had been fasting. At night he changed his clothes. The caravan was traveling in the desert with Joseph's shirt hidden among the grain. It neared the old man's estate. He gesticulated in his room, and then he prayed a long time, lifting his hands to heaven and sniffing the air. He was weeping as the shirt was nearing him.

And when the caravan departed, their father said: "I do indeed feel the smell of Joseph, if only you think me not a dotard (a person who has weakness of mind because of old age)."

They said: "By Allah! Certainly, you are in your old error."

Then, when the bearer of the glad tidings arrived, he cast the shirt over his face, and he became clear sighted. He said: "Did I not say to you, I know from Allah that which you know not.""

They said: "O our father! Ask Forgiveness from Allah for our sins, indeed we have been sinners."

The story began with a dream and it ends with the interpretation of the dream. Almighty Allah narrated: He said: "I will ask my Lord for forgiveness for you, verily, He! Only He is the Oft-Forgiving, the Most Merciful."

Then, when they entered unto Joseph, he betook his parents to himself and said: "Enter Egypt, if Allah will, in security."

And he raised his parents to the throne and they fell down before him prostrate. And he said: "O my father! This is the interpretation of my dream of old! My Lord has made it come true!

(Joseph's dream: He saw eleven stars and the sun and the moon. He saw them prostrating themselves to him. The eleven stars are his brothers, and the suns and the moon are his parents.)

Allah indeed was good to Joseph, when He took Joseph out of prison, and brought his family all to Joseph out of the Bedouin life, after Satan had sown enmity between him and his brothers.

Certainly, the Lord is the Most Courteous and Kind unto whom He will. Truly He! Only He is the All Knowing, the All-Wise."

Consider his feelings now that his dream has come true. He prays to Allah: "My Lord! You have indeed bestowed on me of the sovereignty, and taught me the interpretation of my dreams; the only Creator of the heavens and the earth! You are my Wali (Protector, Helper, Supporter, Guardian etc.). In this world and in the Hereafter, cause me to die as a Muslim (the one submitting to Your Will), and join me with the righteous."

Joseph arranged an audience with the king for himself and his family, to ask the king's permission for them to settle in Egypt. Joseph was an asset to the kingdom, and the king was happy to have him remain with his household. Joseph prostrated to Allah in gratitude.

Before he died, Jacob (peace be upon him) advised his children to adhere to the teachings of Islam, the religion of all of Allah's prophets. Allah the Almighty revealed; Or were you witnesses when death approached Jacob? When he said unto his sons: "What will you worship after me?" they said: "We shall worship your Ilah (God-Allah) the Ilah (God) of your father. Abraham, Ishmael, Isaac, One Ilah (God), and to Him we submit in Islam."

Joseph (peace be upon him), at the moment of his death, asked his brothers to bury him beside his forefathers if they were to leave Egypt. So when Joseph (peace be upon him) passed away, he was mummified and placed in a coffin until such a time as he could be taken out of Egypt and buried beside his forefathers, as he had requested. It was said that he died at the age of one hundred ten.

Prophet Shuaib

The Orator of the Prophets

Prophet Shuaib was an eloquent orator. His proofs were strong, for he spoke in the name of truth and justice. He spoke in the language of pure nature. He calmly talked about corrupt markets and cheating in buying and selling.

The holy Prophet said: Shuaib wept so much out of love of God that he went blind. God restored his sight. But he continued weeping so much that he went blind again. God restored his sight again until when he went blind for the fourth time, God said: O Shuaib! How long are you going to weep? If you fear the fire of hell, I have spared you and if you have a desire for paradise, I have made it permissible to you.

Shuaib said: O my lord and Master! You know that I am not weeping for fear of hell or desire of paradise, rather I am weeping for Your love tied in my heart.

The first person who initiated scales and measure was Prophet Shuaib who made them with his own hands.

God said to the people of Madyan (Madian), We sent you brother Shuaib.

Shuaib said: "O my people! Worship Allah alone, you have no other God but Him."

First, Prophet Shuaib prohibited them from cheating in business by decreasing the weights whenever they gave (products) to people. He commanded them to give just measure and weight whether they were giving or receiving (in transactions). He also forbade them from causing mischief and corruption in the land. This was due to their practice of highway robbery along the roads.

However, the chiefs of the town said: "We shall certainly drive you out from our town and all your friends and followers. If you follow Shuaib then you will be the losers!"

Shuaib said: "O my people! I have conveyed my Lord's Messages to you and I have given you good advice. "

The people of Madyan lived in the country of Ma'an, part of which today is greater Syria. They were a greedy people who did not believe that Allah existed and they led wicked lives.

They always gave short measure. They praised their goods beyond their worth, and hid their defects. They also lied to their customers, thereby cheating them.

He said: "My Lord is the Best Knower of what you do."
God sent His Prophet Shuaib (peace be upon him) armed with many miracles.

Shuaib preached to them, begging them to be thoughtful of Allah's favors.

Shuaib also warned them of the consequences of their evil ways, but they only mocked him.

Shuaib remained calm as he reminded them of his kinship to them and that what he was doing was not for his personal gain.

However, they seized the belongings of Shuaib and his followers, then kicked them out of the city.

They said: "Shuaib you are only one of those bewitched! You are but a human being like us, and we think that you are one of the liars! So cause a piece of heaven to fall on us, if you are of the truthful!"

The Messenger turned to his Lord for help, and his plea was answered. Allah sent down on them scorching heat and they suffered terribly. On seeing a cloud gathering in the sky, they thought it would bring cool, refreshing rain, and rushed outside in the hope of enjoying the rainfall, instead the cloud burst, hurling thunderbolts and fire. They heard a thunderous sound from above which caused the earth under their feet to tremble. The evil doers perished in this state of horror.

Prophet Job (Ayyub)

A Patient and Faithful Servant

Prophet Job (peace be upon him) was one of the descendants of the Prophet Ibrahim (peace be upon them). Prophet Job was a nephew of Prophet Yaqub (peace be upon him). He was sent to reform the people who lived in the desert situated in the north eastern corner of Palestine. When Job was chosen to be the Prophet, he started to teach the people about God and His religion. He advised the people to do good and shun evil. As usual with all the Prophets very few people believed in him in the beginning but gradually the number of his followers began to increase.

It was said, also that his Job's father was one who believed in Abraham (peace be upon him) when he was cast into the fire. Prophet Job (peace be upon him) was a prosperous man with firm faith in Allah. He possessed vast farms, enormous wealth, many cattle and valuable property but these things did not make him arrogant. His wealth provided him with a medium by means of which he sought Allah's grace.

Job was very patient. He suffered from a number of calamities but did not utter a single word of complaint. One day his big farm was attacked by the thieves. They killed many of his servants and carried away forcibly all his cattle. Job did not feel sorry at this loss and thanked Allah. After some time the roof of the house fell down and many members of his family were crushed. Job was much shocked but he held fast to his faith in Allah. He neither shed a tear nor heaved a sigh. He prostrated before the Almighty.

Job remarked that possessions and children were the gifts from Allah. If He had taken His things, it was useless to lament over their loss. After a few years Job suffered from skin disease. His parts of body were covered with loathsome sores. He had many ugly looking ulcers on his face and hands. The sores were full of worms. It is narrated that he picked up those worms which fell from his abscess and praised Allah for creating them.

Above all, his false friends attributed his calamities to his sins. They ridiculed and looked down upon him. All the persons deserted him with the exception of his faithful wife, Rahima. She also grew tired of him in the long run and prayed for his death.

She cursed her husband for retaining integrity in Allah. When Job (peace be upon him) was in an extremely pathetic condition he prayed:

"Truly adversity has afflicted me and You are Most Merciful of all who show mercy."

Allah accepted his prayer. The Holy Quran affirms:

"Then We heard his prayer and removed that adversity from which he suffered, and We gave him his household and the like thereof along with them, a mercy from Our store and remembrance for the worshippers." Job was repentant, remembering Allah with thankfulness, patience, and steadfastness. This was the cause of his rescue and the secret of Allah's praising him.

Allah turned to him with mercy. He was commanded to strike the earth with his foot. He complied with the order and water from the spring gushed forth. He took a bath with the water and got cured from his evil disease. After this he was restored to prosperity. Job (peace be upon him) knelt and prayed expressing a deep sense of gratitude to Allah. He never forgot His favours, mercy and love.

Job was one of the celebrated Prophets. His example illustrates: that those who remain patient under the stress of all circumstances, are never deprived of high rewards. The Holy Quran affirms:

"And surely we try you with something of fear and hunger, and loss of wealth and crops, but give glad-tidings to the steadfast, who when a misfortune befalls them, say lo! We are Allah's (possession of Allah) and to Him shall we surely return. · Such are they on whom are blessings from their Lord, and mercy. Such are the rightly-guided."

A group of angels were discussing Allah's other human creatures, how those who were humble earned Allah's pleasure, while those who were arrogant incurred His displeasure. One of the angels remarked: "The best creature on earth today is Job, a man of noble character who displays great patience and always remembers his Generous Lord. He is an excellent model for the worshippers of Allah.

In return, his Lord has blessed him with a long life and plenty of servants, as well as the needy and the poor share in his good fortune; he feeds and clothes the poor and buys slaves to set them free. He makes those who receive his charity feel as if they are favoring him so kind and gentle is he."

Satan overhearing all of this, became annoyed. He planned to tempt Job to corruption and disbelief, so he hastened to him. He tried to distract Job from his prayers by whispering him about the good things in life but Job was a true believer and would not let evil thoughts tempt him. This disturbed Satan even more; thus he began to hate Job even more.

Satan complained to Allah about Job. He said that although he was continuously glorifying Allah he was not doing so out of his sincerity but to satisfy Allah so that his wealth should not be taken away. It was all a show, all out of greed. "If You remove his wealth then You will find that his tongue will no longer mention Your name and his praying will stop."

Allah told Satan that Job was one of His most sincere devotees. He did not worship Him because of the favors; his worship stemmed from his heart and had nothing to do with material things. But to prove to Satan the depth of Job's sincerity and patience, Allah allowed him to do whatever he and his helpers wished with Job's wealth.

Satan was very happy. He gathered his helpers and set about destroying Job's cattle, servants and farms until he was left with no possessions. Rubbing his hands in glee, Satan appeared before Job in the guise of a wise old man and said to him: "All your wealth is lost, some people say that it is because you gave too much charity and that you are wasting your time with your continuous prayers to Allah. Others say that Allah has brought this upon you in order to please your enemies. If Allah had the capacity to prevent harm, then He would have protected your wealth."

True to his belief, Job replied: "What Allah has taken away from me belongs to Him. I was only its trustee for a while. He gives to whom He wills and withholds from whom He wills." With these words, Job again prostrated to his Lord.

When Satan saw this, he felt frustrated, so he again addressed Allah: "I have stripped Job of all his possessions, but he still remains grateful to You. However he is only hiding his disappointment, for he places great store by his many children. The real test of a parent is through his children. You will see how Job will reject You."

Allah granted Satan authority but warned him that it would not reduce Job' faith in His Lord nor his patience.

Satan again gathered his helpers and set about his evil deeds. He shook the fountain of the house in which Job's children were living and sent the building crashing, killing all of them. Then he went to Job disguised as a man who had come to sympathize with him. In a comforting tone he said to Job: "The circumstances under which your children died were sad. Surely, your Lord is not rewarding you properly for all your prayers." Having said this, Satan waited anxiously hoping Job was now ready to reject Allah. But again Job disappointed him by replying: "Allah sometimes gives and sometimes takes. He is sometimes pleased and sometimes displeased with our deeds. Whether a thing is beneficial or harmful to me, I will remain firm in my belief and remain thankful to my Creator." then Job prostrated to his Lord. At this Satan was extremely vexed.

Satan called on Allah. "O my Lord, Job's wealth is gone, his children are dead, and he is still healthy in body, and as long as he enjoys good health he will continue to worship You in the hope of regaining his wealth and producing more children. Grant me authority over his body so that I may weaken it. He will surely neglect worshipping You and will thus become disobedient."

Allah wanted to teach Satan a lesson that Job was a devoted servant of his Lord so He granted Satan his 3rd request but placed a condition: "I give you authority over his body but not over his soul, intellect or heart, for in these places reside the knowledge of Me and My religion."

Armed with this new authority, Satan began to take revenge on Job's body and filled it with disease until it was reduced to mere skin and bone and he suffered severe pain. But through all the suffering Job remained strong in his faith, patiently bearing all the hardships without complaining. Allah's righteous servant did not despair or turn to others for help but remained hopeful of Allah's mercy. Even close relatives and friends deserted him. Only his kind, loving wife stayed with him. In his hour of need, she showered her kindness on him and cared for him. She remained his sole companion and comforter through the many years of suffering. No one felt sympathy for him except his wife. She took good care of him, knowing his former charity and pity for her.

Satan became desperate. He consulted his helpers, but they could not advise him. They asked: "How is it that your cleverness cannot work against Job, yet you succeeded in misleading Adam the father of man, out of Paradise?"

So Satan went to Job's wife in the form of a man. "Where is your husband?" he asked her.

She pointed to an almost lifeless form crumbled on the bed and said: "There he is, suspended between life and death."

Satan reminded her of the days, when Job had good health, wealth and children. Suddenly, the painful memory of years of hardship overcame her, and she burst into tears. She said to Job: "How long are you going to bear this torture from our Lord? Are we to remain without wealth, children or friends forever? Why don't you call upon Allah to remove this suffering?"

Job sighed, and in a soft voice replied: "Satan must have whispered to you and made you dissatisfied. Tell me how long did I enjoy good health and riches?"

She replied: "80 years."

Then Job replied: "How long am I suffering like this?"

She said: "7 years."

Job then told her: "In that case I am ashamed to call on my Lord to remove the hardship, for I have not suffered longer than the years of good health and plenty. It seems your faith has weakened and you are dissatisfied with the fate of Allah. If I ever regain health, I swear I will punish you with a hundred strokes! From this day onward, I forbid myself to eat or drink anything by your hand. Leave me alone and let my Lord do with me as He pleases."

Crying bitterly and with a heavy heart, she had no choice but to leave him and seek shelter elsewhere. In this helpless sate, Job turned to Allah, not to complain but to seek His mercy: "Verily! Distress has seized me and You are the Most Merciful of all those who show mercy."

So We answered his call, and we removed the distress that was on him, and We restored his family to him (that he had lost), and the like thereof along with them as a mercy from Ourselves and a Reminder for all who worship Us."

Almighty Allah also instructed: "Remember Our slave Job, when he invoked His Lord saying: "Verily! Satan has touched me with distress (by losing my health) and torment (by losing my wealth)!" Allah said to him: "Strike the ground with your foot: This is a spring of water to wash in and cool and a refreshing drink." And We gave him back his family, and along with them the like thereof as a Mercy from Us, and a reminder for those who understand. Job obeyed and almost immediately his good health was restored. Meanwhile, his faithful wife could no longer bear to be parted from her husband and returned to him to beg his forgiveness, desiring to serve him. On entering her house, she was amazed at the sudden change: Job was again healthy! She embraced him and thanked Allah for His mercy.

Job was not worried, for he had taken an oath to punish her with a hundred strokes if he had regained health but he had no desire to hurt her. He knew if he did not fulfill the oath, he would be guilty of breaking a promise to Allah. Therefore in His wisdom and mercy, Allah came to the assistance of His faithful servant and advised him: "take in your hand a bundle of thin grass and strike therewith your wife, and break not your oath." Truly! We found him patient. How excellent a slave! Verily, he was ever oft returning in repentance to Us!"

Prophet Muhammad (peace be upon) said: "While Job was naked, taking a bath, a swarm of gold locusts fell on him, and he started collecting them in his garment. His Lord called him: "O Job! Have I not made you too rich to need what you see?" He said: "Yes, My Lord! But I cannot shun Your Blessings."

Prophets Moses (Musa) and Aaron (Harun)
Faithful and Noble Servants

When Prophet Yusuf (peace be upon him) and his family settled in Egypt, they were called the Israelites. Gradually they increased in number and gained considerable power. These Israelites did not intermingle with other native people. They remained isolated and were considered as foreigners in Egypt.

At that time Egypt was ruled by the king Firaun (Pharaoh). He was arrogant, tyrant and powerful. He thought himself to be god. In Firaun's kingdom the people led miserable lives. They were forced to work as slaves. They were chained and whipped if they refused to work. The Israelites were looked down upon in that society. They suffered badly due to destitution and indigence. Some of them grew weak and died of starvation.

When Pharaoh noticed that the Israelites were increasing in number, he was much alarmed. He held discussions with his counselors on this topic. They decided that Israelites should be snubbed. They should not be allowed to become powerful and supreme in the land. They planned to oppress and persecute them in different ways.

The Pharaoh also ordered that all male children born in the families of the Israelites should be put to death.

When the people heard those terrible orders they were much upset. The soldiers started complying with the orders of their king. Whenever they got wind of the male baby born to any family, they would yank him out of his mother's arms. They did not care for the feelings of the crying mothers. They used to throw the infants mercilessly into the river. It was an awful act of cruelty but no one dared to disobey the orders of Pharaoh because everyone was much scared of him. Many innocent babies were drowned in this way and numerous unfortunate parents expressed lamentations over the death of their dear ones.

In that era one of the Israelite woman gave birth to a male baby who was extremely beautiful. The mother thought that the soldiers of Pharaoh would soon find him out. They would throw him to the fish in the river. God revealed to her to be patient and not to be frightened.

The newly born baby was named Moses (Musa). He was very attractive. His mother fed and concealed him for a few months. When she was unable to hide him any longer, God guided her to cast him into the river. God told her not to grieve, because Moses will be returned to her and He will make him one of the apostles

A wise man said to Pharaoh: "If the children of Israel are all killed, the Pharaoh will lose the manpower of those who work for him. It is better to slaughter them in one year, but to spare them the next year." The Pharaoh liked this solution. Moses' mother was pregnant with Aaron in a year that boys were spared. During a year in which boys were to be slain, she gave birth to Moses. She received a divine revelation to cast Moses into the river.

When the Prophet Musa (peace be upon him) had attained the age of a few months, his mother got made a very tight box. She put a blanket in the box. She lifted her affectionate son and kissed him again and again. She put him in the box with tears in her eyes. Her heart was beating violently. She pushed the box into the water when it was still dark. The box moved slowly on the surface of the water. His sister watched the box at a distance but the mother went back home wailing and sobbing. She was full of anxiety due to the separation of her beloved baby.

Prophet Moses' sister was hiding from place to place along the shore of the river. She was constantly watching the box and praying for the safety of her brother. The box went on moving and gradually came near the shore. Some People were washing their clothes at the shore. By chance they saw the box floating slowly. They waded through the water and picked up the box. They were greatly surprised to see a beautiful infant enclosed in the box. He had a smiling face.

The people took the box to Pharaoh and his family. All of them were full of excitement. Prophet Moses' sister followed them but no one recognized her. The wife of Pharaoh fell in love with the baby. She decided to make him her own son:

Prophet Moses (peace be upon him) became awfully hungry. He began to cry out of hunger. The baby was handed over to a woman who was appointed to nurse him. He did not take her breast and kept on weeping. Everyone was in a fix what to do. The sister of Prophet Moses (peace be upon him) who was standing near remarked: May I bring a woman whom the baby requires?

She was directed to go immediately and call her. She rushed towards her house and informed her mother of the whole situation. She requested her mother to accompany her to Pharaoh's house. Prophet Moses (peace be upon him) was still crying due to hunger. The mother gave him her breast. He was much pleased and drank milk to his heart's content. Pharaoh's wife requested the mother of Prophet Musa (peace be upon him) to stay with them and nurse him.

The Holy Quran states:

"So We restored him to his mother that her eyes might be refreshed and that she might not grieve and that she might know that the promise of Allah is true but most of them do not know."

Prophet Moses (peace be upon him) was brought up in Pharaoh's house like a prince. His mother was taking care of him and he was the apple of her eye. Moses learnt a great deal about Pharaoh and his bad ways of life. He came to know about his cruel treatment towards Israelites. Although he led a luxurious life yet deep inside his heart he had pains.

One day Moses saw an Israelite fighting hard with one of the men of the Pharaoh. They were shouting and hitting each other. Moses appeared on the scene. He tried to pacify them. When he saw that the Egyptian was not going to spare him in spite of several requests, he lifted up his stick and hit the man of the Pharaoh. The man became dizzy and fell to the ground with a bang. Prophet Moses and his companions stepped forward to support the man but he was limp like a rag. Soon after he passed away.

Prophet Moses (peace be upon him) felt sorry for what had happened. It was an accidental and not intentional act. One blow of the stick is quite insufficient to cause the death of a person. His head was twirling. He called his action as a devil's doing who misled human beings. He realized his mistake and prayed for Divine protection.

Soon the news of the murder of a man spread far and wide. The people flew into a rage. They hatched a plan to kill Moses. He became scared and was directed to migrate to another place. Moses packed up his luggage and left Pharaoh's house in the pitch dark when everyone was enjoying a sound sleep. He reached Madian after a long tiresome journey. He sat down to take rest near a watering place.

Moses saw two young girls waiting at a distance. Their sheep were standing near the spring for drinking water. Moses thought that the girls needed some help. Although he was tired and hungry yet he wished to help them. He went up to the girls and asked if they needed help. The girls were modest and bashful. They said that they were waiting so that the shepherds might go away.

Moses drove the sheep to the spring to drink water. It was a kind act of. The girls expressed a deep sense of gratitude for this favor. They took their sheep and proceeded towards their house. Moses went back to rest. He became depressed and prayed to Almighty Allah to help him. In the meanwhile two women came to him and said:

"My father invites you so that he may give you the reward of your having watered for us."

Moses accompanied them. When be entered the house, he introduced himself politely; Soon after he dined with the members of the family. Moses was asked to stay with them. The time passed on happily.

One day the master of the house said:

"I want you to marry one of these two daughters of mine, but you should serve me for eight years but if you complete ten, it will be of your own free will, and I do not wish to be hard on you."

According to the agreement Prophet Moses (peace be upon him) got married to one of the girls of that family. He took care of the farm and the sheep efficiently. Moses had been away from his family for many years. He missed his kith and kin. One day he set out on a journey from Madian. His family accompanied him.

Moses crossed the sandy desert and reached the mountain, Tur. He perceived a brilliant light from a distance. Moses thought that to be fire land and so he reached near it to warm himself. All of a sudden a voice was-heard from the right side of the Valley. It uttered:

"Surely. I am your Lord: so put off your shoes because you are in the sacred Valley which is blessed twice I have chosen you; Verily, I am Allah, there is no god but I, therefore serve-Me-and keep up prayers for My remembrance."

Moses was puzzled and scared. The thing which looked like fire was not fire in the real sense of the word but it was the reflection of the glory of God. It was a moment of great honor for Prophet Moses (peace be upon him).

God commanded Prophet Moses to throw the stick that was in his hand on the ground. He threw the stick in compliance with the orders. To his surprise he saw the stick moving like a long wiggling snake and it greatly scared him. He thought that it was going to bite him. God directed the Moses not to lose courage and pick up the snake. He obeyed and caught hold of the terrible looking snake. When he touched it, it was restored to its former shape. Moses was much amazed to see those happenings.

Soon afterwards God ordered Moses to thrust his hand into his armpit. He did so. When he took out his hand, it was shining white when he put his hand back into his armpit and pulled it out it had been changed into its normal position.

Allah, the Almighty made Moses to perform those miracles so that he might feel better and become sure of the existence of Allah and His power. He was going to derive benefits out of such miracles in future. Allah commanded Moses to go to Egypt to deliver the Israelites from Pharaoh and reform his depraved people. Moses was not good at arguing. He had an impediment in his tongue to speak freely. He sought permission from Allah to take his brother Prophet Aaron (Harun) with him as an aider because he was an eloquent speaker. The permission was immediately granted.

Moses settled with his family in Egypt. They went to Pharaoh to argue with him. They conveyed him the message of Allah but he made fun of them. He did not lose heart and kept on preaching.

The king and his people were not convinced. Finally in desperation, Moses said: O' King! Do you like me to show you that my message is true?

He replied in affirmative with an unbelieving smile on his face. Moses (peace be upon him) threw his stick on the ground and it changed its shape as a terrible looking snake. The people were wonder-struck and got scared of it. When Moses picked it up, it became a stick again. Everyone was much amazed.

Then Moses put his hand in his armpit. When he got it out, his hand was shining brilliantly. The Holy Quran states: "Then he threw down his staff and lo! It was an obvious serpent. And he drew forth his hand and lo! It appeared white to the beholders."

The Chiefs said that Moses was an enchanter. He intended to turn the minds of the people. Pharaoh was much worried. He feared lest people should begin to follow him. He fixed a special day for contest between Moses and other magicians. He sent collectors in various parts of the country to bring enchanters to hold competition and prevail upon Moses. He promised to reward the winners.

On the appointed day thousands of people gathered there. There was a great deal of excitement. Everyone was eager to see the performances of the magicians of the king and the miracles of Prophet Moses (peace be upon him). First of all the royal magicians threw their sticks. They moved and looked like snakes from a distance.

They deceived the eyes of the people and frightened them. The people were much surprised. They appreciated the magicians for their astonishing performances.

Soon after Moses threw his stick. The stick became a hungry serpent by the order of Allah. It wiggled and moved like a dart. It devoured every moving stick that the magician had thrown. The spectators were much impressed. Some of the priests thought that such miracles could be done only by the order of Allah. Most of the magicians drew back humiliated and prostrated themselves adoring. They said: We believe in the Lord of the Worlds; the Lord of Prophet Moses and Prophet Aaron (peace be upon them).

On seeing this state of affairs Pharaoh was much worried. He became mad with rage because his men were inclined to follow the Prophet Musa peace be upon him) and adopt his new religion. He threatened them of dire consequences. He said:

"I shall certainly cut off your hands and your feet on opposite side, then I will crucify you altogether.

Pharaoh and his men began to persecute the followers of Prophet Musa (peace be upon him). The Israelites remained patient. They began to worship and glorify God in their homes. They kept praying to God.

When the Israelites were under the burden of hardships and sufferings, Allah ordered Moses to leave the area with his followers. He promised to save them. In compliance with the Commandment of Allah Moses directed his people to migrate secretly to another place.

When it was dark, a scanty band of the Israelites left Egypt. They took all precautionary measures to escape from the eye-sight of the guards. They moved as fast as they could with firm conviction that they would he saved by Allah. Next day the residence of the Israelites were found desolate and without hustle and bustle.

Pharaoh was informed. He lost his temper and sent heralds to chase the absconders. He wanted to take revenge of his disgrace. He ordered his soldiers to arrest the Israelites and bring them back. When the followers of Prophet Moses (peace be upon him) were near the sea-shore, they heard the sound of the hoofs of their horses. They were much frightened. They thought that they would be overtaken and punished by the enemies.

When the Prophet Musa (peace be upon him) and his followers were being chased Allah revealed this order to him:

"Strike the sea with the rod; and it clove asunder and each part become like a large mountain."

The water of the sea went up high with the great uproar. The bottom of the sea turned into dry land. It was an amazing miracle.

The people could hardly believe their eyes. The Israelites ran desperately and went far ahead. Pharaoh and his huge army chased them in hostility. There was a great uproar again. The water from both the sides poured. It rushed over Pharaoh and his soldiers. They were completely drowned.

The body of Firaun is still present in the Egyptian Museum as an admonitory sign to those who are transgressors.

When Prophet Moses (peace be upon him) and the thousands of his followers got rid of Pharaoh, they expressed a deep sense of gratitude to Allah. They had witnessed an impressive miracle. Now they were free to live according to the teachings of Allah.

Allah commanded Moses to go to a certain mountain for austerity. He had to stay there for forty days. During this period Allah, the Almighty gave a lot of religious knowledge to Moses. He gave him the tablets which contained Ten Commandments. One day he (Musa) said:

"My Lord! Show me Thyself so that I may look upon Thee. He said': you cannot bear to see Me but look at the mountain, if it remains firm in its place, then you will see Me. When his Lord manifested His glory to the mountain He made it crumble and Musa fell down in swoon. When he recovered, he said: Glory be to You: I turn to You and! I am the first of believers".

At the end of the appointed time, Moses went to his people to tell them about the revelations which he had received.

Moses was saddened to see that his followers had become addicted to praying to the cow instead of Allah. Whenever his brother Prophet Aaron (peace be upon him) forbade them to do so, they made fun of him. Sometimes they tortured him.

Moses hard to uproot this form of idolatry from the hearts of the Israelites. Some men who had gone astray, repented but most of them insisted on worshipping a cow.

One season came there was hardly any rain. It overtook the people with draughts and diminution of fruit. There was an acute shortage of water and food. The people began to die of starvation. Moses (peace be upon him) prayed to Allah and He provided them with eatables. Water was not available in the area. They approached Moses for help. He prayed to Allah for a miracle. Allah directed the Prophet to hit a special high cliff with his stick.

Moses touched the cliff saying: By the name of our Lord, Almighty Allah. At once the water gushed forth. There were twelve places in that cliff from which sprang out cool clear water. The people were much amazed at the sight of this wonderful miracle.

The Israelites were of twelve branches each a descendant of a son of Prophet Yaqub (peace be upon him). So each branch came to drink from one of the springs of water from that cliff. The people drank water to their hearts content. They did not have to shove and push for the water because Allah gave them twelve springs.

After staying in the desert for some time Moses planned to proceed towards the blessed land, Palestine. Moses sent twelve men in advance to go and had a bird's eye view of the blessed land. They came back after many days. They told him that there were fertile farms and green trees. There was plenty of water. It made every one eager to go there. It was also reported that the owners of the blessed land were strong and brave. They had invincible armies. It was impossible to capture that land without fighting.

The Israelites were much terrified because they were weak and armless. Moses and a small group of Israelites wished to fight tooth and nail whereas most of them did not agree to fight. Some of them said to Moses You go with your God and fight them. We will stay here and wait.

As the years passed, they increased in number. They gained strength gradually. They formed a small army of their own and marched with faith in their hearts towards the rich blessed land. They fought hard and became victorious in the battle. The inhabitants of that land (the Palestinians) lived with them in peace and harmony. Allah showered favors on Israelites and the Palestinians and they began to prosper.

Prophet Dhu'l-Kifl (Ezekiel)
A Prophet of Fortitude

Dhul-Kifl (peace be upon him) was the Prophet of Allah. The Holy Qur'an has made mention of him in the following two Verses:

And Ismail and Idris and Dhul-kifl; all were men of constancy and patience. We admitted them into out mercy because they were of the righteous ones.

He was so called because he had to do double the work of the Prophets of his time.

He is identified with Ezekiel who was carried away to Babylon after the destruction of Jerusalem. He was chained and imprisoned. He bore all hardships with patience and continued reproving the evil sin of the Bani Israel. When Prophet Ezekiel (peace be upon him) grew old, he wished to appoint a suitable person as his successor to guide the Israelites. He declared: Only that person will be considered competent to become his successor who observes fast during the day and remembers Allah throughout the night and refrains from flying into a rage. One among the crowd stood up and said: (I will adhere to all these conditions. The Prophet Ezekiel (peace be upon him) repeated these conditions thrice and the same person promised solemnly to fulfil the conditions. Thereupon he was appointed as a vicegerent.

After some time he was subjected to a trial. One day Satan in the disguise of an old man knocked at his door. He was allowed to get in. The visitor lodged a complaint against the cruel treatment of the people towards him. The vicegerent directed him to come in the evening. He assured the visitor that all his grievances shall be redressed. He promised but did not turn up at the appointed time. Next day he came again and complained as usual. The vicegerent commanded him to come in the evening. He made a solemn promise to come but did not abide by it. On the third day he came again and knocked at the door but it was not opened. Satan in the disguise of an old man managed to slip into the room and presented himself before the vicegerent. He was wonder-struck at the sudden appearance of the old man. The vicegerent interrogated the visitor. He admitted that he was Satan who assumed the likeness of an old man and was trying to enrage him. He tried to make him back out of his promise but failed in his mission. Thereupon the vicegerent became known as Dhul-kifl because he maintained his solemn promise with the

Prophet Ezekiel (peace be upon him). He refrained from losing temper though the Satan left no stone unturned to annoy him. Soon after Allah chose him as His Prophet.

He commanded the Israelites to wage holy war against those who made mischief on the earth and opposed the religion of Allah. His followers, the Israelites refused to carry out his orders because they were afraid of death. As a retaliation for the utter disobedience of the Commandment of Allah and His Prophet, most of the people were overtaken by calamity. Plague broke out and numerous people died miserably. They deserted their houses in terror and ran away to save their lives. When they covered some distance, they heard a dreadful sound and the death prevailed over them. The corpses were putrefied in the scorching heat of the sun.

When Prophet Dhul-kifl (peace be upon him) came out of the seclusion after seven days. He was overwhelmed with grief to see the predicament of his followers and supplicated: O' Allah! You have perished my followers. Take pity on them and give them a new life. Allah granted the prayer of His Prophet, the dead persons regained their lives. The Holy Qur'an Affirms:

Have you not thought on those who quitted their dwellings--and they were thousands for fear of death. Allah said to them: Die! Then He restored them to life, for full of bounty towards man is Allah. But most men give not thanks.

Afterwards the Prophet Dhul-kifl (peace be upon him) left his followers and migrated to Babylon. After 75 years, he died there.

Prophet David (Dawud)

A Wise and Valiant Servant

When the two armies faced each other, Goliath challenged any soldier from King Saul's army to single combat, as was the custom of battle in those days. Goliath also wanted to show off his strength. The men were afraid, and no one had enough courage to volunteer. The king offered the hand of his pretty daughter in marriage to the man who would fight Goliath, but even this tempting offer did not change the deadly silence among his soldiers.

Then, to everyone's surprise, a youth stepped forward. A roar of laughter echoed from the enemy's side, and even Saul's men shook their heads. The young man was David (Dawud), from the city of Bethlehem. His elderly father had chosen three of his sons to join Saul's army. He had instructed the youngest one, David, not to take part in the fighting but to help the army in other ways and to report to his father daily on what was happening on the war front.

Although Saul was very impressed by the youth's courage, he said: "I admire your courage, but you are no match for that mighty warrior. Let the strong men come forward." David, however, had already decided and was willing to meet the challenge. Proudly, he told the king that only the day before he had killed a lion which had threatened his father's sheep, and on another occasion he had killed a bear. He asked Saul not to judge him by his appearance, for he feared no man or wild beast.

Saul, surprised by young David's brave stance, agreed: "My brave soldier, if you are willing, then may Allah guard you and grant you strength!"

The king dressed David in battle armor and handed him a sword, but David was not used to wearing battle dress. He felt uncomfortable in it, and it obstructed his movements. He removed the armor, then collected a few pebbles and filled his leather pouch with them. He slung it over his shoulder next to his sling. With his wooden staff in hand, he began to walk towards the enemy.

Saul was worried and asked him how on earth, with a sling and a couple of stones was he going to defend himself against the giant? David replied: "Allah Who protected me from the claws of the bear and the fangs of the lion will certainly protect me from this brute!"

When Goliath set eyes on the lean young man who looked like a boy, he laughed loudly and roared: "Are you out to play war with one of your playmates, or are you tired of your life? I will simply cut off your head with one swipe of my sword!"

David shouted back: "You may have armor, shield, and sword, but I face you in the name of Allah, the Lord of the Israelites, Whose laws you have mocked. Today you will see that it is not the sword that kills but the will and power of Allah!"

So saying, he took his sling and placed in it a pebble from his pouch. He swung and aimed it at Goliath. The pebble shot from the whirling sling with the speed of an arrow and hit Goliath's head with great force.

Blood gushed out, and Goliath thumped to the ground, lifeless, before he had a chance to draw his sword. When the rest of his men saw their mighty hero slain, they took to their heels. The Israelites followed in hot pursuit, taking revenge for their years of suffering at the hands of their enemy, killing every soldier they could lay hands on. In this battle the Israelites regained the glory and honor that had been lost for a long time.

David became a hero overnight. Saul kept his word and married his daughter Michal (Miqel) to the young warrior and took him under his wing as one of his chief advisors.

Almighty Allah declared: So they routed them by Allah's Leave and David killed Goliath, and Allah gave him (David) the kingdom (after the death of Saul and Samuel) and wisdom, and taught him of that which He willed. And if Allah did not check one set of people by means of another, the earth would indeed be full of mischief. But Allah is full of Bounty to the Alamin (mankind, jinns and all that exist).

David became the most famous man among the Israelites. However, he was not inveigled by this; he was not a prisoner of fame or leadership but a prisoner of Allah's love.

Therefore, after killing Goliath he went out into the desert in the company of nature, glorifying Almighty Allah and contemplating His favors. David recited his scripture and glorified Allah while the mountains joined him praise and the birds rallied around him.

David's sincerity was not the only factor responsible for the birds and beasts joining with him in glorifying Allah, nor was the sweetness of his voice. It was a miracle from Allah. This was not his only miracle, for Allah also endowed him with the faculty of understanding the languages of birds and animals.

David (peace be upon him) fasted every other day. Allah's Apostle (peace be upon him): "The most beloved fasting to Allah was the fasting of the Prophet David, who used to fast alternate days. And the most beloved prayer to Allah was the prayer of David, who used to sleep the first half of the night, and pray for one third of it and again sleep for a sixth of it.'"

Abdullah Al-As also narrated: "The Prophet (peace be upon him) said to me: 'I have been informed that you pray all the nights and observe fast all the days; is this true?' I replied: 'Yes.' He said: 'If you do so, your eyes will be weak and you will get bored. So fast three days a month, for this will be the fasting of a whole year. (Or equal to the fasting of a whole year).' I said: 'I find myself able to fast more.' He said: 'Then fast like the fasting of (the Prophet) David (peace be upon him) who used to fast on alternate days and would not flee on facing the enemy.'" **(Sahih Al-Bukhari) ISBN: 978-0-692-88036-4**

Allah granted David great influence. His people had a great number of wars in their time, but they had a problem in that the iron armor was too heavy for the fighter to move and fight as he wished. It is said that David was sitting one day, contemplating this problem while toying with a piece of iron. Suddenly, he found his hand sinking in the iron. Almighty Allah had made it flexible for him: And We made the iron soft for him.

The people praised and loved David. However, the hearts of men are fickle and their memories short. Even great men can feel insecure and become petty-minded. One day David found Saul in a worried state. He sensed something strange in Saul's attitude towards him. That night, when he shared his feeling with his wife, she started to weep bitterly and said: "O David, I will never keep any secrets from you." She told him that her father had become jealous of his popularity and feared that he would lose his kingdom to him. She advised him to be on his guard.

This information shocked David very much. He prayed and hoped that Saul's good nature would overcome the darker side of his character. The following day, Saul summoned David to inform him that Canaan had gathered its forces and would march on the kingdom. He ordered David to advance on them with the army and not to return unless victory was gained.

David sensed that this was an excuse to get rid of him; either the enemy would kill him, or in the thick of battle, Saul's henchmen might stab him in the back. Yet he hastened with his troops to meet the army of Canaan. They fought the Canaanites bravely, without thinking of their own safety. Allah granted them victory, and David lived to return to Saul.

Unfortunately, this only increased Saul's fear, so he plotted to kill David. Such is jealousy that not even a daughter's well-being mattered. Michal learned of her father's plan and hurried to warn her husband. David gathered some food and things, mounted his camel and fled. He found a cave in which he remained hidden for many days. After a time, David's brothers and some citizens joined forces with him.

Saul's position became very weak, for he began to rule with a heavy hand. He ill-treated the learned, tortured the reciters of the Talmud, and terrorized his soldiers. This worsened his position, and his subjects began to turn against him. He decided to go war against David. Hearing this news, David marched to confront Saul's army.

The king's army had traveled a great distance and was overcome by fatigue, so they decided to rest in a valley, where they fell asleep. Quietly, David crept up to the sleeping Saul, removed his spear, and cut off a piece of his garment with the sword. David then awakened the king and told him: "Oh king, you come out seeking me, but I do not hate you, and I do not want to kill you. If I did, I would have killed you when you were asleep. Here is a piece of your garment. I could have hacked your neck instead, but I did not. My mission is that of love, not malice." The king realized his mistake and begged for forgiveness.

Time passed and Saul was killed in a battle in which David did not take part. David succeeded Saul, for the people remembered what he had done for them and elected him king. So it was that David the Prophet was also a king. Allah strengthened the dominion of David and made him victorious. His kingdom was strong and great; his enemies feared him without engaging in war with him.

David had a son named Solomon (Suleiman), who was intelligent and wise from childhood. When the following story took place, Solomon was eleven years old.

One day David, was sitting, as usual, solving the problems of his people when two men, one of whom had a field, came to him. The owner of the field said: "O dear Prophet! This man's sheep came to my field at night and ate up the grapes and I have come to ask for compensation."

David asked the owner of the sheep: "Is this true?" He said: "Yes, sir."

David said: "I have decided that you give him your sheep in exchange for the field."

However, Solomon, to whom Allah had given wisdom in addition to what he had inherited from his father, spoke up: "I have another opinion. The owner of the sheep should take the field to cultivate until the grapes grow, while the other man should take the sheep and make use of their wool and milk until his field is repaired. If the grapes grow, and the field returns to its former state, then the field owner should take his field and give back the sheep to their owner."

David responded: "This is a sound judgment. Praise be to Allah for gifting you with wisdom. You are truly Solomon the Wise."

Prophet David was a just and righteous ruler who brought peace and prosperity to his people, and whom Allah honored as a messenger. He delivered Allah's message to the people through the precious gift of his melodious voice. When he recited the Psalms (Zaboor), it was as if the rest of creation chanted with him; people listened as if in a trance. The messages David delivered are famous and well-remembered. They are known in the Bible as the Psalms or Songs of David.

David divided his working day into four parts: one to earn a living and to rest, one to pray to his Lord, one to listen to the complaints of his people, and the last part to deliver his sermons. He also appointed deputies to listen to his subjects' complaints so that in his absence people's problems might not be neglected.

Although a king, he did not live on the income of his kingdom. Being well-experienced in the craft of weapon-making, he made and sold them and lived on that income.

One day, as David was praying in his prayer niche, he ordered his guards not to allow anyone to interrupt him, but two men managed to enter and disturb him. "Who are you?" he asked. One of the men said: "Do not be frightened. We have a dispute and have come for your judgment."

David said: "What is it?" The first man said: "This is my brother, has ninety nine sheep, and I have one. He gave it to me but took it back." David, without hearing from the other party said: "He did you wrong by taking the sheep back, and many partners oppress one another, except for those who are believers."

The two men vanished like a cloud, and David realized that they were two angels sent to him to teach him a lesson. He should not have passed a judgment without hearing from the opposing party. David sought Forgiveness of his Lord, and he fell down prostrate and turned to Allah in repentance. David worshipped Allah, glorified Him and sang His praise until he died. According to traditions, David died suddenly and was mourned by four thousand priests as well as thousands of people. It was so hot that people suffered from the intensity of the sun. Solomon called the birds to protect David and the people from the sun, and they did so until he was buried. This was the first sign of Solomon's power to be witnessed by the people.

Prophet Solomon (Suleiman)
The Knowledgeable and Gifted

Solomon inherited David's prophethood and dominion. This was not a material inheritance, as prophets do not bequeath their property. It is given away to the poor and needy, not to their relatives.

Prophet Muhammad (peace be upon him) said: "The prophets' property will not be inherited, and whatever we leave is to be used for charity." (Sahih Al-Bukhari) ISBN: 978-0-692-88036-4

And indeed We gave knowledge to David and Solomon, and they both said: "All the praises and thanks be to Allah, Who has preferred us above many of His believing slaves!"

And Solomon inherited (the knowledge of) David. He said: "O mankind! We have been taught the language of the animals, birds, and on us have been bestowed all things. This, verily, is an evident grace (from Allah)."

And there were gathered before Solomon his hosts of jinns and men, and birds, and they were all set in battle order (marching forwards).

After his father's death, Solomon became king. He begged Allah for a kingdom such as none after him would have, and Allah granted his wish. Besides wisdom, Allah had blessed Solomon with many abilities. He could command the winds and understand and talk to birds and animals. Allah directed him to teach both men and jinns to mine the earth and extract its minerals to make tools and weapons. He also favored him with a mine of copper, which was a rare metal in those days.

During his time horses were the common mode of transportation. They were very essential for defense, to carry soldiers and cart provisions and weapons of war. The animals were well cared for and well trained. One day Solomon was reviewing a parade of his stable. The fitness, beauty and posture of the horses fascinated him so much that he kept on stroking and admiring them.

The sun was nearly setting, and the time for the middle prayer was passing by. When he realized this, he exclaimed: "I surely love the finer things of life than the service of my Lord! Return them to me."

Almighty Allah revealed: And to David We gave Solomon. How excellent a slave! Verily, he was ever oft returning in repentance (to Us)!

When there were displayed before him, in the afternoon, well-trained horses of the highest breed. And he said: "Alas! I did love the good (these horses) instead of remembering my Lord (in my 'Asr prayer)" till the time was over, and the sun had hidden in the veil of the night. Then he said: "Bring them (horses) back to me." Then he began to pass his hand over their legs and their necks (till the end of the display).

And indeed We did try Solomon and We placed on his throne Jasadan (a devil, so he lost his kingdom for a while) but he did return (to his throne and kingdom by the Grace of Allah and he did return) to Allah with obedience and in repentance. He said: "My Lord! Forgive me, and bestow upon me a kingdom such as shall not belong to any other after me. Verily, You are the Bestower."

So, We subjected to him the wind, it blew gently to his order whithersoever he willed, and also the devils from the jinns including every kind of builder and diver, and also other bound in fetters.

One day Solomon gathered his army, which had different battalions of men, jinns, birds, and animals. He marched them to the country of Askalon.

While they were passing through a valley, an ant saw the approaching army and cried out to warn the other ants: "Run to your homes! Otherwise, unaware, Solomon and his army might crush you!" Solomon, hearing the cry of the ant, smiled. He was glad that the ant knew him to be a prophet who would not intentionally harm Allah's creation. He thanked Allah for saving the ants' lives.

In Jerusalem, on a huge rock, Solomon built a beautiful temple to draw the people to worship Allah. Today this building is known as "The Dome of the Rock." From there, a large band of followers joined Solomon on pilgrimage to the Holy Mosque in Mecca.

After they had completed their hajj, they traveled to Yemen and arrived in the city of San'a. Solomon was impressed by their clever method of channeling water all over their cities. He was keen to build similar water systems in his own country but did not have enough springs.

He set out to find the hoopoe bird, which could detect water under the ground. He sent signals all over the hoopoe to call on him, but it was nowhere to be found. In anger, he declared that unless the bird had a good reason for its absence, he would punish it severely.

The hoopoe eventually came to Solomon and explained the reason for its delay. "I have discovered something of which you are not aware. I have come from Sheba (Sab'a) with important news." Solomon became curious, and his anger subsided. The bird continued: "Sab'a is ruled by a queen named Bilkis (Bilqis), who has plenty of everything, including a splendid throne. But in spite of all this wealth, Satan has entered her heart and the hearts of her people. She rules their minds completely. I was shocked to learn that they worship the sun instead of Allah the Almighty."

To check the hoopoe's information, Solomon sent a letter to the queen with the bird. He instructed the bird to remain hidden and to watch everything.

The hoopoe dropped the letter in front of the queen and flew away to hide. She excitedly opened and read it: "Verily! It is from Solomon, and verily! It reads: 'In the Name of Allah, the Most Beneficent, and Most Merciful; be you not exalted against me, but come to me as Muslims (true believers who submit with full submission).'"

The queen was very disturbed and hurriedly summoned her advisors. They reacted as to a challenge, for they felt that there was someone challenging them, hinting at war and defeat, and asking them to submit to his conditions.

They told her that they could only offer advice, but it was her right to command action. She sensed that they wanted to meet Solomon's invasion threat with a battle. However, she told them: "Peace and friendship are better and wiser; war only brings humiliation, enslaves people and destroys the good things. I have decided to send gifts to Solomon, selected from our most precious treasure. The courtiers who will deliver the gifts will also have an opportunity to learn about Solomon and his military mighty."

Solomon's reconnaissance team brought him the news of the arrival of Bilkis' messengers with a gift. He immediately realized that the queen had sent her men on a probing mission thus, he gave orders to rally the army. The envoys of Bilqis, entering amidst the well-equipped army, realized that their wealth was nothing in comparison to that of the kingdom of Solomon's palace floors, which were made of sandalwood and inlaid with gold.

They noticed Solomon surveying his army, and they were surprised at the number and variety of soldiers, which included lions, tigers, and birds. The messengers stood in amazement, realizing that they were in front of an irresistible army.

The envoys marveled at the splendor surrounding them. They eagerly presented their queen's precious gifts and told Solomon that the queen wished that he would accept them as an act of friendship. They were shocked by his reaction: he did not even ask to open the covers of the containers! He told them: "Allah has given me plenty of wealth, a large kingdom, and prophethood. I am, therefore, beyond bribery. My only objective is to spread the belief in Tawheed, the Oneness of Allah."

He also directed them to take back the gifts to the queen and to tell her that if she did not stop her kind of worship he would uproot her kingdom and drive its people out of the land.

The queen's envoys returned with the gifts and delivered the message. They also told her of the wonderful things they had seen. Instead of taking offense, she decided to visit Solomon. Accompanied by her royal officials and servants, she left Sheba, sending a messenger ahead to inform Solomon that she was on her way to meet him.

Solomon asked the jinns in his employ whether anyone among them could bring her throne to the palace before she arrived. One of them said; "I will bring it to you before this sitting is over." Solomon did not react to this offer; it appeared that he was waiting for a faster means. The jinns competed with each other to please him. One of them named Ifrit said: "I will fetch it for you in the twinkling of an eye!"

No sooner had this one - who had the knowledge of the Book - finished his phrase than the throne stood before Solomon. The mission had, indeed, been completed in the blinking of an eye.

Solomon's seat was in Palestine, and the throne of Bilqis had been in Yemen, two thousand miles away. This was a great miracle performed by one of those sitting with Solomon.

When Bilqis arrived at Solomon's palace, she was welcomed with pomp and ceremony. Then, pointing to the altered throne, Solomon asked her whether her throne looked like that one. She looked at it again and again. In her mind she was convinced that her throne could not possibly be the one she was looking at, as hers was in her palace; et, she detected a striking similarity and replied: "It is as if it were the very one, and resembles mine in every respect." Solomon judged that she was intelligent and diplomatic.

He then invited her into the great hall, the floor of which was laid in glass and shimmering. Thinking it was water, as she stepped on the floor, she lifted her skirt slightly above her heels, for fear of wetting it. Solomon pointed out to her that it was made of solid glass.

She was amazed. She had never seen such things before. Bilqis realized that she was in the company of a very knowledgeable person who was not only a ruler of a great kingdom but a messenger of Allah, as well. She repented, gave up sun worship, accepted the faith of Allah, and asked her people to do the same.

It was finished; Bilqis saw her people's creed fall apart before Solomon. She realized that the sun which her people worshipped was nothing but one of Allah's creatures.

The sun eclipsed within her for the first time, and her heart was lit by a never fading light, the light of Islam.

Solomon's public work was largely carried out by the jinns. This was a punishment for their sins of making people believe that they were all-powerful, knew the unseen, and could foresee the future. As a prophet, it was Solomon's duty to remove such false beliefs from his followers.

Solomon lived amidst glory, and all creatures were subjected to him. Then Allah the Exalted ordained for him to die. His life and death were full of wonders and miracles; thus, his death harmonized with his life and glory. His death, like his life, was unique.

The people had to learn that the future is known neither by the jinns, nor by the prophets, but by Allah alone. Solomon's effort in this direction did not end with his life, for even his death became an example. He was sitting holding his staff, overseeing the jinns at work in a mine. He died sitting in this position. For a long time no one was aware of his death, for he was seen sitting erect. The jinns continued with their sand toil, thinking that Solomon was watching over them.

Many days later, a hungry ant began nibbling Solomon's staff. It continued to do so, eating the lower part of the staff, until it fell out of Solomon's hand, and his great body fell to the ground. People hurried to him, realizing that he had died a long time ago and that the jinns did not perceive the unseen, for had the jinns known the unseen, they would not have kept working, and thinking that Solomon was alive.

Prophet Elijah (Ilyas)

A Righteous Servant

Prophet Elijah (peace be upon him) has been mentioned three times in the Holy Qur'an: And commemorate Ismail, Elijah and Dhul-kifl; each of them was of the company of! The good. And Zachariah and John and Jesus and Elijah all in the ranks of the righteous; and Ismail and Elijah (Al-Yasa) and Jonas and Lot; each have We preferred above the nations. (To them) and their fathers and progeny and brethren, We chose them and We guided them to a straight way.

One day Prophet Elijah (peace be upon him) passed through the fields while the owner (Al-Yasa) was busy ploughing his land. No sooner had the owner seen the Prophet than he abdicated his own work and approached Prophet Elijah (peace be upon him) in hot haste. Al-Yasa began to follow him.

Prophet Elijah was much surprised and remarked: Why do you accompany me after leaving your own work? Al-Yasa retraced his steps and fetched his ox. He slaughtered it, lit the fire and cooked the beef. He fed Elijah, his companions and many other guests to seek the pleasure of Allah. Prophet Elijah was much pleased with the host for his sincerity, hospitality and righteousness. When Elijah (peace be upon him) was about to depart, Al-Yasa expressed his keen desire to live in the company of his honorable guest during the rest of his life and serve him whole heartedly as a humble servant. As the noble attitude of Al-Yasa had pleased Elijah (peace be upon him), the latter accorded him permission without hesitation.

When Prophet Elijah (peace be upon him) was on his death-bed, he wished to bid him farewell. AL-Yasa was not prepared to leave him. Then Elijah (peace be-upon him) asked him to express any of his desires to be fulfilled. Al-Yasa said: I wish that Allah may bestow blessings upon me in the same way as He has blessed you.

Prophet Elijah (peace be upon him) supplicated and invoked blessings of Allah upon his successor. His prayer was granted. Allah chose Al-Yasa as His Prophet after the death of Elijah (peace be upon him). He derived spiritual magnificence from the company of his guide and became the favorite of Allah.

After some time the inhabitants of that locality gave him a warm reception. At that time they were under the spell of starvation. The land was barren and water was not available. Al-Yasa (peace be upon him) supplicated to Allah to show mercy to the famine-stricken people. His prayer was granted and Allah showered his bounties upon them.

Prophet Jonah (Yunus) and the Whale
A Repentant and Faithful Servant

Prophet Jonah (Yunus) (peace be upon him) also known as Dhan-Nun. When the prophethood was conferred upon him, he was commanded to go the inhabitants of the town of Nineveh for preaching the true faith of God. Nineveh was situated on the right bank of the river Tigris. It was the capital city of Assyria. Its people were arrogant and conceited. They led sinful lives. Prophet Yunus (peace be upon him) tried his best to reform them but they turned a deaf ear to his advice and warnings. Soon he began to feel sad. Consequently human frailty overpowered him. He flew into a rage and invoked Allah's wrath on the people of Nineveh. He became impatient and departed without waiting for further command from Allah. He imagined perhaps God had no power over him.

Hardly had he left the city when the skies began to change color and looked as if they were on fire. The people were filled with fear by this sight. They recalled the destruction of the people of 'Ad, Thamud and Noah. Was theirs to be a similar fate? Slowly faith penetrated their hearts. They all gathered on the mountain and started to beseech Allah for His mercy and forgiveness. The mountains echoed with their cries. It was a momentous hour, filled with sincere repentance. Allah removed His wrath and showered His blessings upon them once again. When the threatening storm was lifted, they prayed for the return of Jonah so that he could guide them.

However, Prophet Yunus (peace be upon him) proceeded towards the sea and took a small ship in the company of other passengers. It sailed all day in calm waters with a good wind blowing at the sails. When night came, the sea suddenly changed. A horrible storm blew as if it were going to split the ship into pieces. The waves looked wild. They rose up as high as mountains then plunged down like valleys, tossing the ship and sweeping over the deck.

The storm continued and the ships' captain asked the crew to lighten the ship's heavy load. They threw their baggage overboard, but this was not enough. Their safety lay in reducing the weight further, so they decided among themselves to lighten their load by removing at least one person. The captain directed: We will make lots with all of the travelers' names. The one whose name is drawn will be thrown into the sea." Jonah knew this was one of the seamen's traditions when facing a storm. It was a strange polytheistic tradition, but it was practiced at that time. And so Jonah's affliction and crisis began.

Here was the prophet, subjected to polytheistic rules that considered the sea and the wind to have gods that riot. The captain had to please these gods. Prophet Jonah (peace be upon him) reluctantly participated in the lot, and his name was added to the other travelers' names. The lot was drawn and "Jonah" appeared. Since they knew him to be the most honorable among them, they did not wish to throw him into the angry sea. Therefore, they decided to draw a second lot. Again Jonah's name was drawn. They gave him a final chance and drew a third lot. Unfortunately for Jonah, his name came up again.

Jonah realized that Allah's hand was in all this, for he had abandoned his mission without Allah's consent. The matter was over, and it was decided that Jonah should throw himself into the water. Jonah stood at the edge of the ship looking at the furious sea. It was night and there was no moon. The stars were hidden behind a black fog. But before he could be thrown overboard, Jonah kept mentioning Allah's name as he jumped into the raging sea and disappeared beneath the huge waves.

When Prophet Jonah (peace be upon him) fell into the water, a whale swallowed Jonah into its furious stomach and shut its ivory teeth on him as if they were white bolts locking the door of his prison. The whale dived to the bottom of the sea, the sea that runs in the abyss of darkness.

The captain said: "We will make lots with all of the travelers' names. The one whose name is drawn will be thrown into the sea." The lot was drawn and "Jonah" appeared. Since they knew Jonah to be the most honorable among them, they decided to draw a second lot. Again Jonah's name was drawn. They gave him a final chance and drew a third lot. Unfortunately for Jonah, his name came up again.

Three layers of darkness enveloped him, one above the other; the darkness of the whale's stomach, the darkness of the bottom of the sea, the darkness of the night. Jonah imaged himself to be dead, but his senses became alert when he found he could move. He knew that he was alive and imprisoned in the midst of three layers of darkness. His heart was moved by remembering Allah. His tongue released soon after saying: La ilaha illa Anta (none has the right to be worshipped but You (O Allah), Glorified (and Exalted) be You (above all that evil they associate with You), Truly, I have been of the wrong doers."

Jonah continued praying to Allah, repeating this invocation. Fishes, whales, seaweeds, and all the creatures that lived in the sea heard the voice of Jonah praying, heard the celebration of Allah's praises issuing from the whale's stomach. All these creatures gathered around the whale and began to celebrate the praises of Allah in their turn, each in its own way and in its own language.

The whale also participated in celebrating the praises of Allah and understood that it had swallowed a prophet. Therefore it felt afraid; however, it said to itself; "Why should I be afraid? Allah commanded me to swallow him."

Allah Almighty saw the sincere repentance of Jonah and heard his invocation in the whale's stomach. Allah commanded the whale to surface and eject Jonah onto an island. The whale obeyed and swam to the farthest side of the ocean. Allah commanded it to rise towards the warm, refreshing sun and the pleasant earth.

Jonah's body was inflamed because of the acids inside the whale's stomach. He was ill, and when the sun rose, its ray burned his inflamed body so that he was on the verge of screaming for the pain. However, he endured the pain and continued to repeat his invocation to Allah.

Almighty Allah caused a vine to grow to considerable length over him for protection. Then Allah Exalted caused Jonah to recover and forgave him. Allah told Jonah that if it had not been for his prayers, Jonah would have stayed in the whale's stomach till the Day of Judgment.

Gradually Jonah regained his strength and found his way to his hometown, Nineveh. He was pleasantly surprised to notice the change that had taken place there. The entire population turned out to welcome him. They informed him that they had turned to believe in Allah. Together they led a prayer of thanksgiving to their Merciful Lord.

Prophet Muhammad (peace be upon him) said: "One should never say I am better than Prophet Jonah (peace be upon him)." **(Sahih Al-Bukhari) ISBN: 978-0-692-88036-4**

Gradually the people of Nineveh again adopted evil ways of life. They indulged in idol-worship and debauchery. And so they were destroyed by the Scythians, a large group of Iranian nomads. Prophet Jonah (peace be upon him) died in Nineveh and was buried there. According to the story of some of the historians his tomb is in the village Halmol about ten miles away from Hebron. Hebron is a Palestinian city located in the southern West Bank, 30 km south of Jerusalem. Nestled in the Judaean Mountains, it lies 930 meters above sea level.

Prophet Zachariah (Zakariyya)
A True Worshipper

Prophet Zakariya (Zachariah) (peace be upon him) was an illustrious Prophet of the Israelites. He was one of the descendants of Prophet Suleiman (peace be upon him). The name of his wife was al-Yashbi' who belonged to the family of Prophet Harun (peace be upon him). Prophet Zakariya (peace be upon him) was the patron of Mary, the mother of Prophet Isa (peace be upon him). He was the trustee of Hekal. He worked as a carpenter and earned his livelihood.

Prophet Zakariya (peace be upon him) continued preaching the religion of Allah even in old age. The Israelites were indulged in mischief. They had not only ignored the teachings of his Prophet but tortured him also. Prophet Zakariya (peace be upon him) did not die a natural death. One day the Israelites decided to put him to death. He hid himself in the covern of the tree. The Jews began to saw that part of the tree. Prophet Zakariya (peace be upon him) did not even utter a faint cry. His body was cut into two pieces.

The years had taken their toll on the Prophet Zakariyah (peace be upon him). He was old and bent with age, in his nineties. Despite his feebleness, he went to the temple daily to deliver his sermons.

Prophet Zakariyah (peace be upon him) was not a rich man, but he was always ready to help those in need. His one disappointment in life was that he had no children, for his wife was barren. This worried him, for he feared there was no one after him to carry out his work. The people needed a strong leader, for it they were left on their own, they would move away from Allah's teachings and change the Holy Laws to suit themselves.

During one of his visits to the temple, he went to check on Mary, who was living in a secluded room of the temple. He was surprised to find fresh out of season fruit in her room. Besides him, no one had entry to her room. When he inquired, she told him that the fruit was from Allah. She found it every morning. But why was he so surprised, she asked him. Did he not know that Allah provides without measure for whom He wills?

This noble girl had opened his eyes to a startling idea. Could he not ask his Lord to bless him with a child in his old age? Even if his wife was past childbearing age, nothing was impossible for his Gracious Lord!

So when he called out his Lord (Allah) - a call in secret, saying: "My Lord! Indeed my bones have grown feeble, and gray hair has spread on my head, O my Lord! Give me from Yourself an heir, - who shall inherit me, and inherit also the posterity of Jacob (inheritance of the religious knowledge and Prophethood, not the wealth, etc.) And make him, my Lord, one with whom You are Well-pleased!"

Then the angels called him, while he was standing in prayer, saying: "Allah gives you glad tidings of John confirming (believing in) the Word from Allah, noble keeping away from sexual relations with women, a Prophet, from among the righteous. His name will be Yahya (John). We have given that name to none before him."

He said: "My Lord! How can I have a son, when my wife is barren, and I have reached the extreme old age."

Allah said: "So (it will be). Your Lord says, It is easy for Me. Certainly I have created you before, when you had been nothing."

Zakariyah said: "My Lord! Appoint for me a sign."

He said: "Your sign is that you shall not speak unto mankind for three nights."

It was said to his son: "O John! Hold fast to the Scripture (The Torah). And We gave him wisdom while yet a child, and pure from sins (John) and he was righteous, and dutiful towards his parents, and he was neither an arrogant nor disobedient (to Allah or to his parents). And peace on him the day he was born, the day he dies, and the day he will be raised up to life again!"

Prophet John (Yahya)

A Compassionate and Righteous Servant

Prophet John (peace be upon him) was born a stranger to the world of children who used to amuse themselves, as he was serious all the time. Most children took delight in torturing animals whereas, he was merciful to them. He fed the animals from his food until there was nothing left for him, and he just ate fruit or leaves of trees.

John loved reading since childhood. When he grew up, Allah the Exalted called upon him: "O John! Hold fast to the Scripture (The Torah)." And We gave him wisdom while yet a child.

Allah guided him to read the Book of Jurisprudence closely; thus, he became the wisest and most knowledgeable man of that time. Therefore, Allah the Almighty endowed him with the faculties of passing judgments on people's affairs, interpreting the secrets of religion, guiding people to the right path, and warning them against the wrong one.

John reached maturity. His compassion for his parents, as well as for all people and all creatures, increased greatly. He called people to repent their sins. There are quite a number of traditions told about John. For example, one time his parents were looking for him and found him at the Jordan River. When they met him, they wept sorely, seeing his great devotion to Allah, Great and Majestic.

According to Malik (a religious scholar), grass was the food of John Ibn Zakariyah, and he wept sorely in fear of Allah. A chain of narrators reported that Idris Al Khawlawi said: "Shall I not tell you he who had the best food? It is John Ibn Zakariyah, who joined the beasts at dinner, fearing to mix with men."

One day, Zakariayah did not see his son for three days. He found him weeping inside a grave which he had dug and in which he resided. "My son, I have been searching for you, and you are dwelling in this grave weeping!" "O father, did you not tell me that between Paradise and Hell is only a span, and it will not be crossed except by tears of weepers?" He said to him: "Weep then, my son." Then they wept together.

Other narrations say that John (peach be upon him) said: "The dwellers of Paradise are sleepless out of the sweetness of Allah's bounty; that is why the faithful must be sleepless because of Allah's love in their hearts. How far between the two luxuries, how far between them?"

They say John wept so much that tears marked his cheeks. He found comfort in the open and never cared about food. He ate leaves, herbs, and sometimes locusts. He slept anywhere in the mountains or in holes in the ground. He sometimes would find a lion or a bear as he entered a cave, but being deeply absorbed in praising Allah, he never heeded them. The beasts easily recognized John as the prophet who cared for all the creatures, so they would leave the cave, bowing their heads.

John sometimes fed those beasts, out of mercy, from his food and was satisfied with prayers as food for his soul. He would spend the night crying and praising Allah for His blessings. When John called people to worship Allah, he made them cry out of love and submission, arresting their hearts with the truthfulness of his words. A conflict took place between John and the authorities at that time. A tyrant king, Herod Antipas, the ruler of Palestine, was in love with Salome, his brother's daughter. He was planning to marry his beautiful niece. The marriage was encouraged by her mother and by some of the learned men of Zion, either out of fear or to gain favor with the ruler.

On hearing the ruler's plan, John pronounced that such a marriage would be incestuous. He would not approve it under any circumstance, as it was against the Law of the Torah. John's pronouncement spread like wildfire. Salome was angry, for it was her ambition to rule the kingdom with her uncle. She plotted to achieve her aim. Dressing attractively, she sang and danced before her uncle. Her arousing Herod's lust. Embracing her, he offered to fulfill whatever she desired. At once she told him: "I would love to have the head of John, because he has defiled your honor and mine throughout the land. If you grant me this wish, I shall be very happy and will offer myself to you." Bewitched by her charm, he submitted to her monstrous request. John was executed and his head was brought to Salome. The cruel woman gloated with delight. But the death of Allah's beloved prophet was avenged. Not only she, but all the children of Israel were severely punished by invading armies which destroyed their kingdom.

Prophet John's (peace be upon him) grave is in Umayyah Mosque in Syria. The Holy Qur'an makes mention of the cruel acts of the Israelites in the following Verses: "As to those who deny the Signs of Allah and in defiance of right, slay the prophets, and slay those who teach just dealing with mankind, announce to them a grievous penalty."

Prophet Jesus (Isa)
The Healer

In many verses of the Glorious Qur'an Allah the Exalted denied the claim of the Christians that He has a son. A delegation from Nagran came to the Prophet Muhammad (peace be upon him). They began to talk about their claim about the Trinity, which is that Allah is three in one, the Father, the Son, and the Holy Spirit, with some disagreement among their sects. That is why Allah affirmed in many verses of the Qur'an that Prophet Jesus (peace be upon him) is a servant of Allah, whom He molded in the womb of his mother like any other of His creatures, and that He created him without a father, as He created Prophet Adam (peace be upon him) without a father and even without a mother.

Remember when the wife of Imran delivered her (child Mary), she said: "O my Lord! I have delivered a female child," and Allah knew better what she delivered, - "and the male is not like the female, and I have named her Mary, and I seek refuge with You (Allah) for her and for her offspring from Satan, the outcast."

So her Lord (Allah) accepted her with goodly acceptance. He made her grow in a good manner and put her under the care of Prophet Zechariah (peace be upon him).

Prophet Zakariyah's (peace be upon him) wife's sister had a daughter named Hannah. She was married to Imran, a leader of the Israelites. For many years, the couple remained childless. Whenever Hannah saw another woman with a child, her longing for a baby increased. Although years had passed, she never lost hope. She believed that one day Allah would bless her with a child, on whom she would shower all her motherly love.

She turned to the Lord of the heavens and the earth and pleaded with Him for a child. She would offer the child in the service of Allah's house, in the temple of Jerusalem. Allah granted her request. When she learned that she was pregnant, she was the happiest woman alive, and thanked Allah for His gift. Her overjoyed husband Imran also thanked Allah for His mercy. However, while she was pregnant her husband passed away. Hannah wept bitterly. Alas, Imran did not live to see their child for whom they had so longed.

Hannah prayed: "O my Lord! I have vowed to You what (the child that) is in my womb to be dedicated for Your services, so please accept this, from me. Verily, You are the All-Hearer, the All Knowing."

Hannah had a big problem in reference to her promise to Allah, for females were not accepted into the temple, and she was very worried. Her sister's husband Zakariyah, comforted her, saying that Allah knew best what she had delivered and appreciated fully what she had offered in His service. She wrapped the baby in a shawl and handed it over to the temple elders. As the baby was a girl, the question of her guardianship posed a problem for the elders. This was a child of their late and beloved leader, and everyone was eager to take care of her. Zakariyah said to the elders: "I am the husband of her maternal aunt and her nearest relation in the temple; therefore, I will be more mindful of her than all of you."

As it was their custom to draw lots to solve disagreements, they followed this course. Each one was given a reed to throw into the river. They had agreed that whoever reed remained afloat would be granted guardianship of the girl. All the reeds sank to the bottom except Zakariyah's. With this sign, they all surrendered to the will of Allah and made him the guardian.

To ensure that no one had access to Mary, Zakariyah built a separate room for her in the temple. As she grew up, she spent her time in devotion to Allah. Zakariyah visited her daily to see to her needs, and so it continued for many years. One day, he was surprised to find fresh fruit, which was out of season in her room. As he was the only person who could enter her room, he asked her how the fruit got there. She replied that these provisions were from Allah, as He gives to whom He wills. Zakariyah understood by this that Allah had raised Mary's status above that of other women.

Thereafter, Zakariyah spent more time with her, teaching and guiding her. Mary grew to be a devotee of Allah, glorifying Him day and night.

Prophet Muhammad (peace be upon him) said: "The best of the world's women is Mary (in her lifetime), and the best of the world's women is Khadija (in her lifetime)." **(Sahih Al-Bukhari) ISBN: 978-0-692-88036-4**

Prophet Muhammad (peace be upon him) said: "Many among men attained perfection but among women none attained perfection except Mary the daughter of Imran, and Asiya the wife of Pharaoh."

Asiya is described in the Quran as the wife of the Pharaoh, who reigned during the time of Moses (Musa). She secretly accepted the message of one God after witnessing the miracle of Moses in her husband's court. Asiya worshipped God in secret and prayed in disguise fearing her husband. She died while being tortured by her husband, who had discovered her praying.

While Mary was praying in her temple, an angel in the form of a man appeared before her. Filled with terror, she tried to flee, praying: "Verily! I seek refuge with the Most Beneficent (Allah) from you, if you do fear Allah."

The angel said: "I am only a Messenger from your Lord, (to announce) to you the gift of a righteous son."

She said: "How can I have a son, when no man has touched me, nor am I unchaste?"

He said: "So (it will be), your Lord said: "that is easy for me (Allah): And (We wish) to appoint him as a sign to mankind and a mercy from Us (Allah), and it is a matter (already) decreed, (by Allah).'"

The angel's visit caused Mary great anxiety, which increased as the months went by. How could she face giving birth to a child without having a husband? Later, she felt life kicking inside her. With a heavy heart, she left the temple and went to Nazareth, the city in which she had been born where she settled in a simple farm house to avoid the public.

But fear and anxiety did not leave her. She was from a noble and pious family. Her father had not been an evil man nor was her mother an impure woman. How could she prevent tongues from wagging about her honor?

After some months, she could not bear the mental strain any longer. Burdened with a heavy womb, she left Nazareth, not knowing where to go to be away from this depressing atmosphere.

She had not gone far (about four to six miles from Jerusalem), when she was overtaken by the pains of childbirth. She sat down against a dry palm tree, and here she gave birth to a son. Looking at her beautiful baby, she was hurt that she had brought him into the world without a father. She exclaimed: "I wish I had died before this happened and had vanished into nothingness!"

Suddenly, she heard a voice nearby: "Grieve not, your Lord has placed a rivulet below, and shake the trunk of this tree, from which ripe dates will fall. So eat and drink and regain the strength you have lost; and be of good cheer, for what you see is the power of Allah, Who made the dry palm tree regain life, in order to provide food for you." For a while she was comforted by Allah's miracle, for it was a sure sign of her innocence and purity.

She decided to return to the city. However, her fears also returned. What was she going to tell the people? As if sharing his mother's worry, the baby began to speak: "If you meet any person say: 'I have vowed to fast for The Beneficent and may not speak to any human today.'" With this miracle, Mary felt at ease.

As she had expected, her arrival in the city with a newborn baby in her arms aroused the curiosity of the people. They scolded her: "This is a terrible sin that you have committed." She put her finger to her lips and pointed to the child. They asked: "How can we speak to a newborn baby?" To their total amazement, the child began to speak clearly: "I am Allah's servant. Allah has given me the Book, and has made me a prophet, and has blessed me wherever I may be, and has enjoined on me prayers and alms-giving as long as I live. Allah has made me dutiful towards she who had borne me. He has not made me arrogant nor unblessed. Peace unto me the day I was born, the day I die, and the day I shall be raised alive."

Most of the people realized that the baby was unique, for it Allah wills something, He merely says "Be" and it happens. Of course, there were some who regarded the baby's speech as a strange trick, but at least Mary could now stay in Nazareth without being harassed.

It was said that Joseph the Carpenter was greatly surprised when he knew the story, so he asked Mary: "Can a tree come to grow without a seed?" She said: "Yes, the one which Allah created for the first time." He asked her again: "Is it possible to bear a child without a male partner?" She said: "Yes, Allah, created Adam without male or female!"

It was also said that, while pregnant, Mary went one day to her aunt, who reported that she felt as if she was pregnant. Mary in turn, said that she, too, was feeling as if she was pregnant. Then her aunt said: "I can see what is in my womb prostrating to what is in your womb."

The Jewish priests felt this child Jesus was dangerous, for they felt that the people would turn their worship to Allah the Almighty Alone, displacing the existing Jewish tenets. Consequently, they would lose their authority over the people. Therefore, they kept the miracle of Jesus's speech in infancy as a secret and accused Mary of a great misdeed.

As Jesus (peace be upon him) grew, the signs of prophethood began to increase. He could tell his friends what kind of supper waited for them at home and what they had hidden and where. When he was twelve years old, he accompanied his mother to Jerusalem. There he wandered into the temple and joined a crowd listening to the lecture of the Rabbis (Jewish priests). The audience were all adults, but he was not afraid to sit with them. After listening intently, he asked questions and expressed his opinion. The learned rabbis were disturbed by the boy's boldness and puzzled by the questions he asked, for they were unable to answer him. They tried to silence him, but he ignored their attempts and continued to express his views. Jesus became so involved in this exchange that he forgot he as expected back home.

In the meantime, his mother went home, thinking that he might have gone back with relatives or friends. When she arrived, she discovered that he was not there, so she returned to the city to look for him. At last she found him in the temple, sitting among the learned, conversing with them. He appeared to be quite at east, as if he had been doing this all his life. Mary got angry with him for causing her worry. He tried to assure her that all the arguing and debating with the learned had made him forgot the time.

Jesus grew up to manhood. It was Sabbath, a day of complete rest: no fire could be lit or extinguished nor could females plait their hair. Moses (peace be upon him) had commanded that Saturday be dedicated to the worship of Allah.

Jesus was on his way to the temple. Although it was the Sabbath, he reached out his hand to pick two pieces of fruit to feed a hungry child. This was considered to be a violation of the Sabbath law. He made a fire for the old women to keep themselves warm from the freezing air. Another violation. He went to the temple and looked around. There were twenty thousand Jewish priests registered there who earned their living from the temple. The rooms of the temple were full of them.

Jesus observed that the visitors were much fewer than the priests. Yet the temple was full of sheep and doves which were sold to the people to be offered as sacrifices. Every step in the temple cost the visitor money. They worshipped nothing but money. In the temple, the Pharisees and Sadducees acted as if it were a market place, and these two groups always disagreed on everything. Jesus followed the scene with his eyes and observed that the poor people who could not afford the price of the sheep or dove were swept away like flies by the Pharisees and Saducees. Jesus was astonished. Why did the priests burn a lot of offerings inside the temple, while thousands of poor people were hungry outside it?

On this blessed night, the two noble prophets John (peace be upon him) and Zakariyah (peace be upon him) died, killed by the ruling authority. On the same night, the revelation descended upon Jesus (peace be upon him). Allah the Exalted commanded him to begin his call to the children of Israel. To Jesus, the life of ease was closed, and the page of worship and struggled was opened.

Like an opposing force, the message of Jesus came to denounce the practices of the Pharisees and to reinforce the Law of Moses. In the face of a materialistic age of luxury and worship of gold, Jesus called his people to a nobler life by word and deed. This exemplary life was the only way out of the wretchedness and diseases of his age. Jesus's call, from the beginning, was marked by its complete uprightness and piety. It appealed to the soul, the inner being, and not be a closed system of rules laid down by society.

Jesus continued inviting the people to Almighty Allah. His call was based on the principle that there is no mediation between the Creator and His creatures. However, Jesus was in conflict with the Jews' superficial interpretation of the Torah. He said that he did not come to abrogate the Torah, but to complete it by going to the spirit of its substance to arrive at its essence.

He made the Jews understand that the Ten Commandments have more value than they imagined. For instance, the fifth commandment does not only prohibit physical killing, but all forms of killing; physical, psychological, or spiritual. And the sixth commandment does not prohibit adultery only in the sense of unlawful physical contact between a man and a woman, but also prohibits all forms of unlawful relations or acts that might lead to adultery. The eye commits adultery when it looks at anything with passion. Jesus was therefore in confrontation with the materialistic people. He told them to desist from hypocrisy, show and false praise. There was no need to hoard wealth in this life. They should not preoccupy themselves with the goods of this passing world; rather they must preoccupy themselves with the affairs of the coming world because it would be everlasting.

Jesus told them that caring for this world is a sin, not fit for pious worshippers. The disbelievers care for it because they do not know a better way. As for the believers, they know that their sustenance is with Allah, so they trust in Him and scorn this world.

Jesus continued to invite people to worship the Only Lord, Who is without partner, just as he invited them to purify the heart and soul.

His teaching annoyed the priests, for every word of Jesus was a threat to them and their position, exposing their misdeeds.

The Roman occupiers had, at first, no intention of being involved in this religious discord of the Jews because it was an internal affair, and they saw that this dispute would distract the Jews from the question of the occupation.

However, the priests started to plot against Jesus. They wanted to embarrass him and to prove that he had come to destroy the Mosaic Law. The Mosaic Law provides that an adulteress be stoned to death. They brought him a Jewish adulteress and asked Jesus: "Does not the law stipulate the stoning of the adulteress?" Jesus answered: "Yes." They said: "This woman is an adulteress." Jesus looked at the woman and then at the priests. He knew that they were more sinful than she. They agreed that she should be killed according to Mosaic Law, and they understood that if he was going to apply Mosaic Law, he would be destroying his own rules of forgiveness and mercy.

Jesus understood their plan. He smiled and assented: "Whoever among you is sinless can stone her." His voice rose in the middle of the Temple, making a new law on adultery, for the sinless to judge sin. There was none eligible; no mortal can judge sin, only Allah the Most Merciful.

As Jesus left the temple, the woman followed him. She took out a bottle of perfume from her garments, knelt before his feet and washed them with perfume and tears, and then dried his feet with her hair. Jesus turned to the woman and told her to stand up, adding: "O Lord, forgive her sins." He let the priests understand that those who call people to Almighty Allah are not executioners. His call was based on mercy for the people, the aim of all divine calls.

Jesus continued to pray to Allah for mercy on his people and to teach his people to have mercy on one another and to believe in Allah.

Jesus continued his mission, aided by divine miracles. Some Qur'anic commentators said that Jesus brought four people back from the dead: a friend of his named Al-Azam, an old woman's son, and a woman's only daughter. These three had died during his lifetime. When the Jews saw this they said: "You only resurrect those who have died recently; perhaps they only fainted." They asked him to bring back to life Sam, the son of Prophet Noah (peace be upon him).

When he asked them to show him his grave, the people accompanied him there. Jesus invoked Allah the Exalted to bring him back to life and behold, Sam came out from the grave gray-haired. Jesus asked: "how did you get gray hair, when there was no aging in your time?" He answered: "O Spirit of Allah, I thought that the Day of Resurrection had come; from the fear of that day my hair turned gray."

Jesus continued calling people to Almighty Allah and laying down for them what might be called "the law of the Spirit." Once when standing on a mountain surrounded by his disciples, Jesus saw that those who believed in him were from among the poor, the wretched, and the downtrodden, and their number was small. Some of the miracles which Jesus performed had been requested by his disciples, such as their wish for a "holy table" to be sent down from heaven.

It was related that Jesus commanded his disciples to fast for thirty days; at the end of it, they asked Jesus to bring food from heaven to break their fast. Jesus prayed to Allah after his disciples had doubted Allah's power. The great table came down between two clouds, one above and one below, while the people watched. Jesus said: "O Lord, make it a mercy and not a cause of distress." So it fell between Jesus's hands, covered with a napkin.

Jesus suddenly prostrated and his disciples with him. They sensed a fragrance, which they had never smelled before. Jesus said: "The one who is the most devout and most righteous may uncover the table, that we might eat of it to thank Allah for it." They said: "O Spirit of Allah, you are the most deserving."

Jesus stood up, then performed ablution and prayed before uncovering the table, and behold, there was a roasted fish. The disciples said: "O Spirit of Allah, is this the food of this world or of

Paradise?" Jesus said to his disciples: "Did not Allah forbid you to ask questions? It is the divine power of Allah the Almighty Who said: 'Be,' and it was. It is a sign from Almighty Allah warning of great punishment for unbelieving mortals of the world. This is the kernel of the matter."

It is said that thousands of people partook of it, and yet they never exhausted it. A further miracle was that the blind and lepers were cured.

The Day of the Table became one of the holy days for the disciples and followers of Jesus. Later on, the disciples and followers forgot the real essence of the miracles, and so they worshipped Jesus as a god.

Jesus went on his mission, but the forces of evil accused him of magic, infringement of the Mosaic Law, allegiance with the devil; and when they saw that the poor people followed him, they began to scheme against him.

The Sanhedrin, the highest judicial and ecclesiastical council of the Jews, began to meet to plot against Jesus. The plan took a new turn. When the Jews failed to stop Jesus's call, they decided to kill him. The chief priests held secret meetings to agree on the best way of getting rid of Jesus. While they were in such a meeting, one of the twelve apostles of Jesus, Judas Iscariot, went to them and asked: "What will you give me if I deliver him to you?" Judas bargained with them until they agreed to give him thirty pieces of silver known as shekels. The plot was laid for the capture and murder of Jesus.

It was said that the high priest of the Jews tore his garment at the meeting, claiming that Jesus had denied Judaism. The tearing of clothes at that time was a sign of disgust.

The priests had no authority to pass the death sentence at that time, so they convinced the Roman governor that Jesus was plotting against the security of the Roman Empire and urged him to take immediate action against him. The governor ordered that Jesus be arrested. According to the Book of Matthew, Jesus was arrested and the council of the high priests passed the death sentence upon him. Then, they began insulting him, spitting on his face and kicking him.

It was the Roman custom for the condemned to be flogged before they were executed. So Pilate, the Roman governor, ordered that Jesus be flogged. The Mosaic Law stipulates forty lashes, but the Roman had no limit, and they were brutal lashes. After that, Jesus was handed to the soldiers for crucifixion. They took off his clothes, and kept them. They put a crown of thorns on his head to mock him. According to custom he carried his cross on his back to increase his suffering.

Finally, they reached a place called Golgotha, meaning the Place of Skulls, outside the walls of Jerusalem. Instead of giving him a cup of wine diluted with scent to help lessen the pain on the cross, the soldiers gave Jesus a cup of vinegar diluted with gall. Then they crucified him and, as a further mockery, two thieves with him. So it is written in the Bible.

But the faith of Islam came with views quite different from that of the extend gospels with regards to both the end of Jesus and his nature. The Glorious Qur'an affirms that Allah the Exalted did not permit the people of Israel to kill Jesus or crucify him. What happened was that Allah saved him from his enemies and raised him to heaven. They never killed Jesus, they killed someone that resembled him.

Allah the Almighty declared: And because of their saying (in boast), "We killed Messiah Jesus, son of Mary, the Messenger of Allah," but they killed him not, nor crucified him, but the resemblance of Jesus was put over another man (and they killed that man) and those who differ therein are full of doubts. They have no certain knowledge, they follow nothing but conjecture. For surely; they killed him not (Jesus, son of Mary): But Allah raised him (Jesus) up (with his body and soul) unto Himself (and he is in the heavens). And Allah is Ever All Powerful, All Wise.

Say: (O Muhammad): "He is Allah, the One. Allah As-Samad (The Self-Sufficient Master, Whom all creatures need, He neither eats nor drinks). He begets not, nor was He begotten; and there is none co-equal or comparable unto Him."

Prophet Muhammad
The Seal of the Prophets

Prophet Muhammad (peace be upon him) was born in Mecca, Saudi Arabia, on Monday, 12 Rabi' Al-Awal (2 August A.D. 570). His mother was Aminah. His father, 'Abdullah, was the son of Abdul Muttalib. His genealogy has been traced to the noble house of Ishmael, the son of Prophet Abraham in about the fortieth descend.

Prophet Muhammad (peace be upon him) became an orphan quickly. His father died before his birth, and before he was six years old his mother died. The doubly orphaned Muhammad (peace be upon him) was put under the charge of his grandfather Abdul Muttalib who took the tenderest care of him. But then the old chief died two years afterwards. On his deathbed he confided to his son Abu Talib the charge of the little orphan.

When Muhammad (peace be upon him) was twelve years old, he accompanied his uncle Abu Talib on a mercantile journey to Syria, and they proceeded as far as Busra. The journey lasted for some months. It was at Busra that the Christian monk Bahira met Muhammad. He is related to have said to Abu Talib: 'Return with this boy and guard him against the hatred of the people, for a great fate awaits your nephew."

After this journey, the youth of Muhammad (peace be upon him) seems to have been passed uneventfully, but all authorities agree in ascribing to him such correctness of manners and purity of morals as were rare among the people of Mecca. The fair character and the honorable bearing of the unobtrusive youth won the approbation of the citizens of Mecca, and by common consent he received the title of "Al Ameen," The Faithful.

In his early years, Prophet Muhammad (peace be upon him) was not free from the cares of life. He had to watch the flocks of sheep of his uncle, who, like the rest of the Bani Hashim, had lost the greater part of his wealth. From youth to manhood he led an almost solitary life. The lawlessness rife among the Meccans, the sudden outbursts of causeless and bloody quarrels among the tribes of Quraish, naturally caused feelings of pity and sorrow in the heart of the sensitive youth.

When Prophet Muhammad (peace be upon him) was twenty five years old, he traveled once more to Syria as a factor of a noble and rich Quraishi widow named Khadijah; and, having proved himself faithful in the commercial interests of that lady, he was soon rewarded with her hand in marriage. This marriage proved fortunate and singularly happy. Khadijah was much the senior of her husband, but in spite of the disparity of age between them, the tenderest devotion on both sides existed. This marriage gave him the loving heart of a woman who was ever ready to console him in his despair and to keep alive within him the feeble, flickering flame of hope when no man believed in him and the world appeared gloomy in his eyes.

When Muhammad reached thirty-five years, he settled by his judgment a big dispute. In rebuilding the Sacred House of the Ka'ba in A.D. 605, the question arose as to who should have the honor of raising the black stone, the most holy relic of that House, into its proper place. Each tribe claimed that honor. The senior citizen advised the disputants to accept for their arbitrator the first man to enter from a certain gate. The proposal was agreed upon, and the first man who entered the gate was Prophet Muhammad (peace be upon him). His advice satisfied all the contending parties. He ordered the stone to be placed on a piece of cloth and each tribe to share the honor of lifting it up by taking hold of a part of the cloth. The stone was thus deposited in its place, and the rebuilding of the House was completed without further problems.

Prophet Muhammad (peace be upon him) being rather rich at this time, tried to discharge part of the debt of gratitude and obligation which he owed to his uncle by undertaking the bringing up and education of his son 'Ali. A year later he adopted 'Akil, another of his uncle's sons.

Khadijah bore Muhammad (peace be upon him) three sons and four daughters. However, all sons died in childhood, but in loving 'Ali he found much consolation.

About this time, Muhammad set a good example of kindness, which created a salutary effect upon his people. His wife Khadijah had made him a present of young slave named Zaid Ibn Haritha, who had been brought as a captive to Mecca and sold to Khadijah. When Zaid was "a very young boy, he accompanied his mother on a visit to her family. While they were staying with the Maan tribe, horsemen from the Qayn tribe raided their tents and kidnapped Zayd. They took him to the market and sold him as a slave for 400 dinars, but Prophet Muhammad (peace be upon him) took Zaid by the hand and led him to the black stone of Ka'ba, where he publicly adopted him as his son. Henceforward Zaid was called the son of Muhammad.

Prophet Muhammad (peace be upon him) was now approaching his fortieth year, and his mind was ever-engaged in profound contemplation and reflection. For years after his marriage, Muhammad had been accustomed to secluding himself in a cave in Mount Hira, a few miles from Mecca. To this cave he used to go for prayer and meditation, sometimes alone and sometime with his family. There, he often spent the whole nights in deep thought and profound communion with the Unseen yet All-Knowing Allah of the Universe. It was during one of those retirements and in the still hours of the night, when no human sympathy was near, that an angel came to him to tell him that he was the Messenger of Allah sent to reclaim a fallen people to the knowledge and service of their Lord. Angel Gabriel (Jibreel) (peace be upon him) appeared to him and said: "Read!" But as Muhammad was illiterate, having never received any instruction in reading or writing, he said to the angel: "I am not a reader." The angel took a hold of him and squeezed him as much as he could bear, and then said again: "Read!" Then Prophet said: "I am not a reader." The Angel again seized the Prophet and squeezed him and said: "Read! In the Name of Your Lord, Who has created (all that exists). Read! And your Lord is the Most Generous, Who has taught (the writing) by the pen, has taught man that which he knew not."

Then Prophet Muhammad (peace be upon him) repeated the words with a trembling heart. He returned to Khadijah from Mount Hira and said: "Wrap me up! Wrap me up!" She wrapped him in a garment until his fear was dispelled. He told Khadijah what had occurred and that he was becoming either a soothsayer or one smitten with madness. She replied: "Allah forbid! He will surely not let such a thing happen, for you speak the truth, you are faithful in trust, you bear the afflictions of the people, you spend in good works what you gain in trade, you are hospitable and you assist your fellow men. Have you seen anything terrible?" Muhammad replied: "Yes," and told her what he had seen. Whereupon, Khadijah said: "Rejoice, O dear husband and be cheerful. He is Whose hands stands Khadijah's life bears witness to the truth of this fact, that you will be the prophet to this people."

At the beginning of his mission, Prophet Muhammad (peace be upon him) opened his soul only to those who were attached to him and tried to free them from the gross practices of their forefathers. After Khadijah, his cousin' Ali was the next companion.

After 'Ali, Muhammad's adopted son Zaid became a convert to the new faith. He was followed by Abu Bakr, a leading member of the Quraish tribe and an honest, wealthy merchant who enjoyed great consideration among his compatriots. He was but two years younger than the Prophet. His adoption of the new faith was of great moral effect. Soon after, five notables presented themselves before the Prophet and accepted Islam. Several converts also came from lower classes of the Arabs to adopt the new religion.

For three weary long years, Prophet Muhammad (peace be upon him) labored very quietly to deliver his people from the worship of idols. Polytheism was deeply rooted among the people. It offered attractions, which the new faith in its purity did not possess. The Quraish had personal material interests in the old worship, and their prestige was dependent upon its maintenance. Amidst all these trials the Prophet (peace be upon him) did not waver. He was full of confidence in his mission, even when on several occasions he was put in imminent danger of losing his life.

The Prophet (peace be upon him) continued preaching to the Arabs in a most gentle and reasonable manner. As the number of believers increased and the cause of the Prophet was strengthened by the conversions of many powerful citizens, the Prophet's preaching alarmed Quraish. Their power and prestige were at stake. They were the custodians of the idols, which the Prophet had threatened to destroy; in fact their existence and living wholly depended upon the maintenance of the old institutions. The Prophet taught that in the sight of his Lord all human were equal, the only distinction recognized among them being the weight of their piety.

During this period, 'Umar Al-Khattab adopted Islam. In him the new faith gained a valuable adherent and an important factor in the future development and propagation of Islam. Umar had been a violent opposer of the Prophet and a bitter enemy of Islam. His conversion is said to have been worked by the miraculous effect on his mind of a Surah, Taha, of the Quran which his sister was reading in her house, where he had gone with the intention of killing her for adopting Islam. Umar struck his sister in her face. The blow caused her mouth to bleed. He was going to strike again but the sight of blood made him pause. He suddenly appeared to relent, and then in a changed tone asked her to show him what she was reading. She sensed a change in him but said: "You are an unclean idolater, and I cannot allow you to touch the Word of God."

Umar immediately went away, washed himself, returned to his sister's home, please read the text of the Qur'an that you were reading. His sister read to him: **"When the sun is overthrown, And when the stars fall, And when the hills are moved, And when the camels big with young are abandoned, And when the wild beasts are herded together, And when the seas rise, And when souls are reunited, And when the girl-child that was buried alive is asked For what sin she was slain, And when the pages are laid open, And when the sky is torn away, And when hell is lighted, And when the Garden is brought nigh, (Then) every soul will know what it hath made ready. Oh, but I call to witness the planets, the stars which rise and set, and the close of night, and the breath of morning, That this is in truth the word of an honored messenger."**

Umar then immediately went to the house of Arqam where he formally accepted Islam. Umar's conversion to Islam took place at the close of the sixth year of the Prophet's mission.

In the twelfth year of his mission, the Prophet made his night journey from Mecca to Jerusalem, and thence to heaven. His journey, known in history as Miraj (Ascension) was a real bodily one and not only a vision. It was at this time that Allah ordered the Muslims to pray the five daily prayers.

Almighty Allah had said: Glorified (and Exalted) be He (Allah) (above all that evil they associate with Him), Who took His slave Muhammad for a journey by night from AL Masjid al Haram (at Makka) to the farthest mosque (in Jerusalem), the neighborhood whereof We have blessed, order that We might show him (Muhammad) of Our Ayat (proofs, evidences, lessons, signs, etc.). Verily, He is the All Hearer, the All Seer."

Abbas Ibn Malik reported that Malik Ibn Sasaa said that Allah's Messenger described to them his Night Journey saying: "While I was lying in Al-Hatim or Al-Hijr, suddenly someone came to me and cut my body open from here to here." I asked Al-Jarud, who was by my side, "What does he mean?" He said: "It means from his throat to his public area," or said, "From the top of the chest." The Prophet further said, "He then took out my heart. Then a gold tray of Belief was brought to me and my heart was washed and was filled (with Belief) and then returned to its original place. Then a white animal which was smaller than a mule and bigger than a donkey was brought to me." (On this Al-Jarud asked: "Was it in the Buraq, O Abu Hamza?" I (Anas) replied in the affirmative. The Prophet said: "The animal's step (was so wide that it) reached the farthest point within the reach of the animals' sight. I was carried on it, and Gabriel set out with me till we reached the nearest heaven.

"When he asked for the gate to be opened, it was asked, 'Who is it?' Gabriel answered, 'Gabriel.' It was asked, 'Who is accompany you?' Gabriel replied, 'Muhammad.' It was asked, 'Has Muhammad been called?' Gabriel replied in the affirmative. Then it was said. 'He is welcomed. What an excellent visit his is!' The gate was opened, and when I went over the first heaven, I saw Adam there. Gabriel said to me: 'This is your father, Adam; pay him your greetings.' So I greeted him and he returned the greetings to me and said: 'You are welcomed, O pious son and pious Prophet.' Then Gabriel ascended with me till we reached the second heaven. Gabriel asked for the gate to be opened. It was asked: 'Who is it?' Gabriel answered: 'Gabriel.' It was asked: 'Who is accompany you?' Gabriel replied, 'Muhammad.' It was asked: 'Has he been called?' Gabriel answered in the affirmative. Then it was said: 'He is welcomed. What an excellent visit his is!' The gate was opened.

"When I went over the second heaven, here I saw John (Yahya) and Jesus (Isa), who were cousins of each other. Gabriel said to me: "these are John and Jesus; pay them your greetings.' So I greeted them and both of them returned my greetings to me and said, 'You are welcomed, O pious brother and pious Prophet.' Then Gabriel ascended with me to the third heaven and asked for its gate to be opened. It was asked 'Who is it?' And Gabriel replied: 'Gabriel.' It was asked, 'Who is accompany you?' Gabriel replied, 'Muhammad.' It was asked, 'Has he been called?' Gabriel replied in the affirmative. Then it was said: 'He is welcomed, what an excellent visit his is!' The gate was opened, and when I went over the third heaven there I saw Joseph (Yusuf), Gabriel said to me: 'This is Joseph, pay him your greetings.' So I greeted him and he returned the greetings to me and said: 'You are welcomed, O pious brother and pious Prophet.' Then Gabriel ascended with me to the fourth heaven and asked for its gate to be opened. It was asked 'Who is it?' Gabriel replied, 'Gabriel' It was asked: 'Who is accompany you?' Gabriel replied: 'Muhammad.' It was asked: 'Has he been called?' Gabriel replied in the affirmative. Then it was said: 'He is welcomed, what an excellent visit his is!'

"The gate was opened, and when I went over the fourth heaven, there I saw Enoch (Idris), Gabriel said to me: 'This is Enoch; pay him your greetings.' So I greeted him and he returned the greetings to me and said: 'You are welcomed O pious brother and pious Prophet.'

Then Gabriel ascended with me to the fifth heaven and asked for its gate to be opened. It was asked: 'Who is it?' Gabriel replied: 'Gabriel.' It was asked: 'Who is accompany you?' Gabriel replied 'Muhammad.' It was asked: 'Has he been called?' Gabriel replied in the affirmative. Then it was said: 'He is welcomed, what an excellent visit his is!' So when I went over the fifth heaven, there I saw Aaron (Harun), Gabriel said to me: "this is Aaron; pay your greetings.' So I greeted him and he returned the greetings to me and said: "You are welcomed, O pious brother and pious Prophet." The Gabriel ascended with me to the sixth heaven and asked for its gate to be opened. It was asked: 'Who is it?' Gabriel replied: 'Gabriel.' It was asked: 'Who is accompanying you?' Gabriel replied: 'Muhammad.' It was said: 'Has he been called?' Gabriel replied in the affirmative. It was said: 'He is welcomed. What an excellent visit his is!'

"When I went over the sixth heaven, there I saw Moses (Musa). Gabriel said to me: "This is Moses; pay him your greeting. So I greeted him and he returned the greetings to me and said: "You are welcomed, O pious brother and pious Prophet." When I left him (Moses) he wept. Someone asked him: 'What makes you weep?' Moses said: 'I weep because after me there has been sent (as Prophet) a young man whose followers will enter Paradise in greater numbers than my followers.'

Then Gabriel ascended with me to the seventh heaven and asked for its gate to be opened. It was asked: 'Who is it?' Gabriel replied: 'Gabriel.' It was asked: 'Who is accompanying you?' Gabriel replied: 'Muhammad.' It was asked: 'Has he been called?' Gabriel replied in the affirmative. Then it said: 'He is welcomed. What an excellent visit his is!'

"So when I went (over the seventh heaven), there I saw Abraham (Ibrahim). Gabriel said to me: 'This is your father; pay your greetings to him.' So I greeted him and he returned the greetings to me and said: 'You are welcomed, O pious son and pious Prophet.' Then I was made to ascend to Sidrat-ul-Muntaha (the Lote Tree of the utmost boundary). Behold! Its fruits were like the jars of Hajr (a place near Medina) and its leaves were as big as the ears of elephants. Gabriel said: "this is the Lote Tree of the utmost and boundary.' Behold! There ran four rivers, two were hidden and two were visible, I asked: 'What are these two kinds of rivers, O Gabriel?' He replied: 'As for the hidden rivers, they are two rivers in Paradise and the visible rivers are the Nile and the Euphrates.'

"Then Al-Bait-ul-Ma'mur (the Sacred House) was shown to me and a container full of wine and another full of milk and a third full of your followers are following.' Then the prayers were enjoined on me: they were honey were brought to me. I took the milk. Gabriel remarked: 'this is the Islamic religion which you and fifty prayers a day. When I returned, I passed by Moses, who asked me; 'What have you been ordered to do?' I replied: 'I have been ordered to offer fifty prayers a day.' Moses said: 'Your followers cannot bear fifty prayers a day, and by Allah I have tested people before you, and I have tried my level best with Bani Israel in vain. Go back to your Lord and ask for reduction to lessen your followers'' burden.'

So I went back, and Allah reduced ten prayers for me. Then again I came to Moses, but he repeated the same as he had said before. Then again I went back to Allah, and He reduced ten more prayers. When I came to Moses he said the same. I went back to Allah, and He ordered m to observe ten prayers a day. When I came back to Moses, he repeated the same advice, so I went back to Allah and was ordered to observe five prayers a day.

"When I came back to Moses, he said: 'What have you been ordered?' I replied: 'I have been ordered to observe five prayers a day.' He said: 'Your followers cannot bear fear prayers a day, and no doubt, I have got an experience of the people before you, and I have tried my level best with Bani Israel, so go back to your Lord and ask for reduction to lesson your followers' burden.' I said: 'I have requested so much of my Lord that I feel ashamed, but I am satisfied now and surrender to Allah's Order.' When I left, I heard a voice saying: 'I have passed My order and have lessened the burden of My worshippers.'"

The Meccans began to think seriously of killing Prophet Muhammad (peace be upon him). A number of noble youths were selected for the bloody deed. As the night advanced, the assassins posted themselves round the Prophet's dwelling. They watched all night long, waiting to murder the Prophet (peace be upon him) when he should leave his house at the early dawn. However, the Prophet Muhammad (peace be upon him) was warned of the danger, and he directed 'Ali to lie down in his place and wrap himself up in his green clock, which he did. The Prophet miraculously escaped through the window and he repaired to the house of Abu Bakr, unperceived by door.

The killers looked through a crevice and saw 'Ali, but they mistook for the Prophet Muhammad (peace be upon him). So they continued watching there until morning. When 'Ali arose, they found themselves deceived. The fury of the Quraish was now unbounded. The news that the would be assassins had returned unsuccessful and that the Prophet Muhammad (peace be upon him) had escaped aroused their whole energy. A price of a hundred camels was set upon Muhammad's head.

"One day, while we were sitting in Abu Bakr's house at noon, someone said to Abu Bakr: 'This is Allah's Messenger with his head covered coming at a time at which he never used to visit us before.' So Allah's Messenger came and asked permission to enter, and he was allowed to enter. When he entered, he said: 'I have been given permission to migrate.' Abu Bakr said: 'Shall I accompany you? 'Allah's Messenger said: 'Yes.' Abu Bakr said: ' take one of these two she-camels of mine.' Allah's Messenger replied: 'I will accept it with payment.' So we prepared the baggage quickly and put some journey food in a leather bag for them. Asma, Abu Bakr's daughter, cut a piece from her waist belt and tied the mouth of the leather bag with it, and for that reason she was named 'Dhat-un-Nitaqain' (the owner of two belts).

"Then Allah's Messenger and Abu Bakr reached a cave on the mountain of Thaur and they stayed there for three nights. When the Muslims of Medina heard the news of the departure of Allah's Messenger from Mecca (towards Medina), they started going to the Harra every morning. They would wait for him till the heat of the noon forced them to return. One day, after waiting for a long while, they returned home, and when they went into their houses, a Jew climbed up to the roof of one of the forts of his people to look for something, and he saw Allah's Messenger and his companions, dressed in white clothes, emerging out of the desert mirage. The Jew could not help shouting at the top of his voice: 'O you Arabs! Here is your great man whom you have been waiting for!' So all the Muslims rushed to their arms and received Allah's Messenger on the summit of Harra.

Allah's Messenger prayed then mounted his she-camel and proceeded on, accompanied by the people till his she-camel knelt down at the place of the Mosque of Allah's Messenger at Medina. Some Muslims used to pray there in those days, and that place was a yard for drying dates belonging to Suhail and Sahl, the orphan boys who were under the guardianship of Asad In Zurara. When his she-camel knelt down, Allah's Messenger said: 'This place, Allah willing, will be our abiding place.' Allah's Messenger then called the two boys and told them to suggest a price for that yard so that he might take it as a mosque. The two boys said: 'No, but we will give it as a gift, O Allah's Messenger!' Allah's Messenger then built a mosque there. The Prophet himself started carrying unburned bricks for its building and while doing so, he was saying: 'This load is better than the load of Khaibar. **(Sahih Al-Bukhari) ISBN: 978-0-692-88036-4**

Thus was accomplished the hijrah, or the flight of Muhammad as called in European annals, from which the Islamic calendar dates.

When the Prophet Muhammad and his companions settled at Yathrib, this city changed its name, and henceforth was called, Al-Medina, Al-Munawara, the Illuminated City, or more shortly, Medina, the City. It is situated about eleven-day's journey to the north of Mecca.

Seven years had already elapsed since the Prophet and his Meccan followers had fled from their birthplace. Their hearts began to yearn for their homes and for their Sacred House the Ka'ba. With the exception of a slight resistance, the Prophet entered Mecca almost unopposed. The city which had treated him so cruelly. Now the Prophet (peace be upon him) entered Mecca on his favorite camel Al Kaswa.

The Muslim army entered the city unpretentiously and peacefully. No house was robbed, no man or woman was insulted. The Prophet granted a general amnesty to the entire population of Mecca. He did however, order the destruction of all idols and pagan images of worship, upon which three hundred and fifty idols which were in the Sacred House of Ka'ba were thrown down.

Thus, the mission of the Prophet Muhammad was now accomplished; the whole work was achieved in his lifetime. Idolatry with its nameless abominations was entirely destroyed. The people who were sunk in superstition, cruelty, and vice in regions where spiritual life was utterly unknown were now united in one bond of faith, hope and charity. The tribes which had been from time immemorial engaged in perpetual wars were now united together by the ties of brotherhood, love, and harmony.

On the return of the sacred month of pilgrimage, the Prophet, under the presentiment of his approaching end, determined to make a farewell pilgrimage to Mecca. In February 632, he left Medina with a very considerable concourse of Muslims. It is stated that from ninety thousand to one hundred and forty thousand people accompanied the Prophet. Before completing all rites of the pilgrimage, he addressed the assembled multitude from the top of Mount Arafat in the following words:

"O people! Listen to my words, for I know not whether another year will be vouchsafed to me after this year to find myself among you. Your lives and property are sacred and inviolable among one another until you appear before the Lord, as this day and this month are sacred for all; and remember, you will have to appear before your Lord Who will demand from you an account for all your actions. O people, you have rights over your wives, and your wives have a right over you. Verily you have taken them on the security of Allah and have made their people lawful unto you by the words of Allah. And your slaves, see that you feed them with such food as you eat yourselves, and clothe them with the stuff you wear, and if they commit a fault which you are not inclined to forgive, then part with them; for they are the servants of the Lord and are not to be harshly treated.

O people, listen to my words and understand them. Know that all Muslims are brothers. Keep yourselves from injustice. Let him who is present tell this to him who is absent. It maybe that he who is told this afterward may remember better than he who has now heard it.

The Prophet concluded his sermon by exclaiming: "O Lord, I have fulfilled my message and accomplished my work." The assembled multitude, all in one voice, cried: "Yea, verily you have." The Prophet again exclaimed: "O Lord, I beseech You, bear witness to it."

Having rigorously performed all the ceremonies of the pilgrimage, that his example might be followed by all Muslims for all succeeding ages, the Prophet returned with his followers to Medina.

The eleventh year of the hijrah, the health of the Prophet grew worse. His last days were remarkable for the calmness and serenity of his mind. He was able, though weak and feeble, to lead the public prayers until within three days of his death. As long as his strength lasted, he took part in the public prayers.

The last time he appeared in the mosque he addressed the congregation, after the usual prayers were over, in the following words: "O Muslims, if I have wronged anyone of you, here I am to answer for it; if I owe anything to anyone, all I may happen to possess belongs to you." A man in the crowd rose and claimed three Dhirhams which he had given to a poor man at the request of the Prophet. They were immediately paid back with these words: "Better to blush in this world than in the next."

The Prophet then prayed and implored Allah's mercy for those who had fallen in the persecution of their enemies. He recommended to all his followers the observance of religious duties and the leading of a life of peace and goodwill. Then he spoke with emotion and with a voice still so powerful as to reach beyond the outer doors of the mosque: "By the Lord in Whose hand lies the soul of Muhammad as to myself, no man can lay hold on me in any matter; I have not made lawful anything excepting what Allah has made lawful; nor have I prohibited anything but that which Allah in His Book has prohibited."

Then turning to the women who sat close by, he exclaimed: "O Fatimah, my, daughter, and Safia, my aunt, work you both that which procure you acceptance with the Lord, for verily I have no power to save you in any wise." He then rose and re-entered the house of Aisha.

After this, the Prophet never appeared at public prayers. A few hours after he returned from the mosque, the Prophet died while laying his head on Aisha. As soon as the Prophet's death was announced, a crowd of people gathered at the door of the house of Aisha, exclaiming: "How can our messenger be dead?" Umar said: "No, he is not dead; he will be restored to us, and those are traitors to the cause of Islam who say he is dead. If they say so let them be cut in pieces."

But Abu Bakr entered the house at this moment, and after he had touched the body of the Prophet with a demonstration of profound affection, he appear at the door and addressed the crowd with the following speech: "O Muslims, if anyone of you has been worshipping Muhammad, then let me tell you that Muhammad is dead. But if you really do worship Allah then know that Allah is living and will never die. Do you forget the verse in the Quran: Muhammad is not more than a Messenger, and indeed (many) Messengers have passed away before him. If he dies or is killed, will you then turn your back on your heels (as disbelievers)? And he who turns back on his heels, not the least harm will he do to Allah, and Allah will give reward to those who are grateful." (Ch 3:144 Quran). Upon hearing this speech of Abu Bakr, 'Umar acknowledged his error, and the crowd was satisfied and dispersed.

Al-Abbas, the Prophet's uncle, presided at the preparation for the burial, and the body was duly washed and perfumed. There was some dispute between the Quraish and the Ansars as to the place of burial; however, Abu Bakr settled the dispute by affirming that he had heard the Prophet say that a prophet should be buried at the very spot where he died. A grave was accordingly dug in the ground within the house of Aisha and under the bed on which the Prophet died. In this grave the body was buried, and the usual rites were performed by those who were present.

Thus ended the glorious life of that Prophet Muhammad. May the peace and blessings of Allah be upon him.

www.ingramcontent.com/pod-product-compliance
Lightning Source LLC
Chambersburg PA
CBHW081403070526
44583CB00020B/2654